Living in
Latin America

Living in Latin America

A Case Study in Cross-Cultural Communication

Raymond L. Gorden

Antioch College

Edited by
H. Ned Seelye

Published by National Textbook Company
in conjunction with the American Council on the Teaching of Foreign Languages

To Charlotte . . .
who in her dual role as wife
and assistant project director
helped beyond the call of duty.

1990 Printing

Published by National Textbook Company, a division of NTC Publishing Group.
© 1974 by NTC Publishing Group, 4255 West Touhy Avenue,
Lincolnwood (Chicago), Illinois 60646-1975 U.S.A.
All rights reserved. No part of this book may be reproduced, stored
in a retrieval system, or transmitted in any form or by any means,
electronic, mechanical, photocopying, recording or otherwise, without
the prior permission of NTC Publishing Group.
Manufactured in the United States of America.
Library of Congress Catalog Card Number: 73-94494

O ML 9 8

Contents

Foreword

This is by far the best guide yet to appear on how to increase the quality of routine interpersonal relations centering around home life in Latin America. An inquisitive sociologist from Antioch College, Raymond L. Gorden, used a magnificently simple technique to find out how young Americans could better adjust to life in Colombian homes—he asked both Americans and Colombians to talk about themselves and each other. This book is the product of more than three years of systematic probing by Dr. Gorden and his staff into cross-cultural communication—and miscommunication—between Americans and Colombians.

One intriguing phenomenon Gorden uncovered in his interviews with Colombians underlines the importance of developing a cultural context for communication. While one cannot penetrate another culture without knowing its language, Gorden discovered that Americans who were fluent in textbook Spanish left more frustrated Colombians in their wake than did Americans who spoke little or no Spanish. How could it have been less exhausting for a Latin American to interact with someone who did *not* speak Spanish than with someone who did? The answer lies in the nature of communication itself.

People communicate by what they say—and by what they do not say. This "silent language," as anthropologist Edward Hall called it, is learned rather unconsciously by us all as we learn to talk and to behave in "appropriate" ways. Most monolingual people do not consciously separate the process of socialization from that of "languaging." For them, learning to read means learning to read English; learning arithmetic means learning that two plus two are four, not *dos y dos son cuatro*. Since our skills in behaving properly and speaking properly are developed simultaneously, we naturally expect someone who talks *as though* he knew how to act indeed to *act* accordingly. No one expects someone who says "Me want fry potat French" to distinguish a salad fork from a demitasse spoon. Colombians, like other people, rightly assume that if a stranger does not know the language he does not know the social conventions either. Conversely, it is also naturally—but falsely—assumed that if someone speaks your language he shares the same extralinguistic referents.

What frustrated the Colombians who interacted with Americans who had learned Spanish in school was the disconcerting absence of shared cultural assumptions. This cultural knowledge is critical if two people are to understand each other. Some specialists of "silent" or "body" language claim that as much as 80 percent of communication occurs nonverbally. This is not to say that language is unimportant to communication—for this would be patently absurd—but rather that it is but one facet of communication. Language fluency by itself is just not enough.

Any communication which is to be sustained across time and varying circumstance must be based on fluency in *both* the language and the nonlinguistic cultural systems of the target peoples. The present book does much to prepare students of Hispanic language and culture to anticipate the source for much of the miscommunication that inevitably results when two people interact who are imperfectly socialized into each other's culture.

An amazing characteristic of second-culture understanding is that it is elusive in even its most obvious manifestations. Gorden tells how even after extended periods of residence in Colombian homes American guests still did not know many culturally appropriate routines: What to do with one's towel after use; where to put one's shoes at night; when and to what extent should one's bedroom door be left open; what responsibilities do maids have; how to ask permission to watch T.V. The misunderstandings provoked by this type of trivial pattern often resulted in Americans not being invited to participate in Colombian social life.

One has to ask to what extent the cultural patterns reported in this book can be generalized beyond Colombia. Gorden, a careful social scientist, is reluctant to claim validity beyond the field setting of his research. The duties of maids in Guatemala are not precisely the same as for maids in Colombia. Any student of culture is faced with a range of behavior that differs from country to country and from social class to social class. Men behave differently from women and older people do not act the same as children. These variables of age, sex, social class, and place of residence necessarily limit the extent to which we can generalize from any pattern of behavior. Fortunately, most of the patterns reported by Gorden recur with surprising frequency throughout the Hispanic world.

Were the reported patterns of only local occurrence, still they might be worthy of scrutiny. There are three tests which can be applied to any cultural fact to help the teacher decide whether it is academically defensible to teach it. First, to what extent will knowing the fact help one predict behavior? Second, to what extent will manipulating the fact develop one's skill in perceiving other patterns that have broad predictive value? And third, to what extent will demonstrating knowledge of the fact enable one to avoid hostility in cross-cultural encounters?

When judged by these criteria, the present book is thrice blessed.

H. NED SEELYE

Preface

I realize that I have neither provided a complete cultural map of even the *bogotano* middle-class family, nor have I built a refined theory of cross-cultural communication in general. Nevertheless, I feel that we have made a step in the direction of demonstrating the importance of the sociocultural setting for interpreting the meaning of verbal or nonverbal messages exchanged in that setting. The need for descriptions of relevant non-linguistic aspects of foreign cultures where Americans go to work is recognized by a growing number. For example, Edward T. Hall points out that he has found it necessary to sell the idea to some foreign service officers who failed to "grasp the fact that there was something really different about overseas operations; that what was needed was something bold and new, not just more of the same old history, economics, and politics." But once the selling job was done, he discovered a more serious problem:

> Those Foreign Service officers and other trainees who did take seriously what they heard and managed to make something out of it came up against another problem. They would say, "Yes, I can see that you have something there. Now I'm going to Damascus. Where can I find something to read that will help me to do business with the Arabs?" *We were stumped!*[1]

Dr. Hall's exclamation, "We were stumped!" expresses the situation with respect to training Peace Corps volunteers for work in Latin America or preparing students to take full educational advantage of their stay in Latin America. This lack was expressed by Jack Vaughn, as he summed up his three years experiences as Director of the Peace Corps:

> The biggest problem facing me as Director has been training and all the things surrounding it—improving it—making it relevant. It is our most glaring deficiency. I haven't solved it and I'm sorry.
>
> Sensitivity training especially is bad. It is shot through with charlatans and worse. And there is no evidence that it has done anybody any good. I have tried to get rid of sensitivity training, but training contractors keep sneaking it in under

other names . . . D-groups, T-groups, Z-groups. I feel that self-discovery should come from doing something practical, from getting out and actually eye-balling a slum dweller.[2]

Both Hall, as anthropologist and consultant to many international projects, and Vaughn, as chief administrator of the Peace Corps, have an acute appreciation of the tremendous gap between the need and the supply of solid information or principles that are relevant in preparing Americans for cross-cultural experience. In the absence of solid information about the sociocultural setting of the type that will help the American communicate and participate better abroad, the vacuum created by the need tends to be filled by "sensitivity training," history, art, and geography. As useful as they may be they are not an adequate substitute for the study of the nonlinguistic barriers to communication between Americans and members of a particular foreign culture.

The writer hopes that this study has made some contribution in this direction by describing, analyzing and interpreting the interaction between young Americans as guests in Colombian homes.

We have tried to *demonstrate* the importance of the situationally determined silent assumptions in the process of cross-cultural communication, *discover* some of the specific nonlinguistic barriers to communication between North Americans and Colombians, and *sensitize* the reader to some of the symptoms and results of communication blockages typical among people in daily cross-cultural contact. The extent to which we have done some of these things for the reader, we will feel successful.

1. Edward T. Hall, *The Silent Language* (New York: Doubleday & Co., 1959), p. 36.
2. Anonymous, "Jack Vaughn Reflects on his Peace Corps Experience," *Peace Corps Volunteer* (May 1969).

Acknowledgments

Unlike research in the physical sciences, studies of human behavior depend directly upon goodwill between the investigator and all the persons involved in the data-collection process. This dependence is most vital in cross-cultural studies where understanding and close cooperation must be developed between members of both cultures who are in several disciplines in order to carry out the investigation.

I feel particularly fortunate to have had the high degree of interest, cooperation, and support of many Colombians in pursuit of objective, but often subtle, information. Although space does not permit me to name everyone who helped the project through its several stages of development, I feel compelled to mention those whose cooperation was most generous and who were most directly connected with the collection and analysis of data used in this particular study.

I would like to acknowledge the help of Dr. Virginia Gutiérrez de Pineda, authority on the Colombian family, who supplied experienced and competent Colombian interviewers; also Dr. Lucy M. Cohen whose bilingual application of her anthropological training was essential in developing the interview guides, helping with field strategy, and criticizing the manuscript. Psychologist Blanca de Nebbia did exploratory interviewing and interpretation of interview data that were essential to the revision of the interview guides used with host families.

Contacts with host families in Bogotá were facilitated by CEUCA (*Centro de Estudios Universitarios Colombo-Americano*), which is administered by Antioch College for the Great Lakes Colleges Association. Additional host families were contacted through Professor Antoine Kattah Fayad and Joseph Spagna of the *Centro de Estudios Latinoamericanos* at the *Universidad Javeriana*, which administers programs for North American students in Bogotá, and also through the cooperation of Sra. Charlotte A. de Samper, Foreign Student Advisor at the *Universidad de los Andes*. Their interest in objectively analyzing the problems of the

American guests in Colombian host homes to improve cross-cultural relations was an essential ingredient in the project.

The interviewers who did the bulk of the field work with the Colombian host families were Rosa Esther Buitrago Dueñas, Carmenza Huyó Sánchez, and Sra. Obdulia Carrillo de Ambrosio—all graduates (*licenciados*) of the *Facultad de Sociología* of the *Universidad Nacional de Colombia*. Sra. Tulia Elvira Ruan de Hanks, in addition to interviewing host families, was invaluable as a translator of the taperecorded interviews and as general public relations assistant.

The processing of the data—including translating, transcribing, content analysis, typing, and reproduction of the final copy—was efficiently and painstakingly carried out by Nohora Romero Baquero, Mary Ann Gómez Fabling, and Meris Isabel Agámez Alvarez. Their efforts were efficiently coordinated with the field team and the many administrative necessities by my wife, Charlotte Gilson Gorden. Dr. John V. Saunders, of the University of Florida, and Dr. Louis Kriesberg, of Syracuse University, served as consultants in the early conceptualization of the problem.

Among the Colombians who carefully read the manuscript and gave critical suggestions were Enrique Corrales, Antoine Kattah, Mario Torres, and Pablo Valencia. Among the North Americans who gave critical suggestions were Victor Ayoub, Lucy Cohen, Bernard Manker, Esther Oldt, and Louis Kriesberg. Any errors or inadequacies that remain are the sole responsibility of the author.

The project depended basically upon the unstinting interest and voluntary assistance of more than 90 Colombian families and 120 American students and Peace Corps trainees who furnished data in many ways: participating in group discussions, collecting information by participant observation, filling out questionnaires, and responding to taperecorded depth interviews.

Finally, the whole project would not have been possible without the funds furnished by the research contract between Antioch College and the U.S. Office of Education. The liaison work with the project was done by Dr. Carl P. Epstein of the Institute for International Studies in the U.S. Office of Education.

1

Introduction

For an American to live with a foreign family for several months of his life is a potential educational experience. Both the guest and host may have moments of discouragement and excitement, of depression and euphoria, of closeness and distance, of conflict and harmony. Neither will be the same after having had the experience. However, this international family-living experience also has the potential for miseducation, as in any attempt to "see" a foreign culture. People may see only what they want to see, or they may see the reflections of their own cultural actions rather than what is there.

Family living provides an inside view of a culture; it allows the stranger to assume a more meaningful role than as a tourist; it provides the additional vantage point of direct *participation in* the culture as a balance to *studying about* it. The people of the host culture can be seen as real human beings rather than statistical abstractions or literary-type characters.

If the American is properly sensitized, living with a foreign family is an experience with basic cross-cultural communication problems. In a very real sense the interpersonal relationship between the American guest and his Colombian host is a microcosm of the cultural component in the international relations between Latin America and the United States.

This is particularly true when the guest and host are middle or upper socioeconomic class, for it is in this social stratum that most international contacts take place.

In addition to becoming acquainted with a group of individuals of a different culture, the experience should also provide insights into the relations between the family and the larger local and national community of which it is a part. In most Latin American countries, the family with its extended kinship network looms larger in the total social organization than in the United States. The kinship system penetrates into business, commerce, education, church, and government more extensively.

This book is a study of the kinds of nonlinguistic communication problems particular Americans had in particular Colombian homes. We are not trying to generalize about the cultural patterns of either North America or Latin America. Yet it does have value beyond the single case. If another foreign culture has some of the same characteristics found in these families, the same potential communication problems exist for Americans. Goodwill, sensitivity, and intelligence are not a substitute for knowledge of the nonlinguistic cultural patterns in cross-cultural communication. The general nature of the cross-cultural communication *process* and the effects of the nonlinguistic patterns, which apply to communication between any two cultures at the abstract level, is the overall focus of this book.

Information was gathered from a total of 106 Colombian *señoras*. They represented households that had had almost 200 American guests during the calendar year. Nineteen of these families had Peace Corps trainees currently, and the other 83 families had undergraduate students from more than 40 colleges and universities in the United States. Since we felt it was particularly important to interview the señoras who might have had serious difficulty with an American guest, we included 15 families who had indicated that they did not care to have an American guest again.

The American college students represented many United States student subcultures. They came from Mennonite colleges; Catholic colleges; small secular colleges; large state universities; and small denominational colleges including Friends, Methodist, Baptist, Dutch Reform, Lutheran, and Presbyterian. Jewish students were mainly from the secular colleges and universities. The students ranged in level from second-semester freshmen to first-semester seniors, with more than 75 percent in the second or third year of college. Their average age was 20.5 years, and the average age of the Peace Corps trainees was 25 years and included three newly married couples.

Some of the American students and Peace Corps trainees interviewed in this study felt that by living with an urban middle-class family they were being deprived of the opportunity to become acquainted with the "real" Colombian—the statistically average rural lower socioeconomic class person. As valuable as it would be to have a better insight into the agrarian family and its milieu, its aspirations and problems, and even recognizing that a few revolutionary leaders such as Zapata and Villa have emerged from the lower class, we should not overlook the fact that the political and economic organizations that profoundly influence the fate of most of the people are in the hands of the upper class who control organizations manned by the middle-class stratum of the urban society. The participants in *international* relations are also recruited from this group.

The objectives of almost all programs for living with a foreign family are the same: The American can obtain a more intimate and realistic view of the foreign family and its cultural milieu, and a feeling of mutual understanding and goodwill will be generated in the experience.

This study sheds some light upon how the attainment of these objectives, which depend upon cross-cultural communication, can be frustrated or facilitated. The three major findings run counter to some of the simplistic commonsense assumptions regarding the nature of the cross-cultural communication process. These major findings, stated briefly, are: (1) Goodwill and intelligence are often helpful but not enough; (2) facility in the foreign language is necessary but not sufficient to guarantee cross-cultural communication; (3) seemingly trivial misunderstandings often lead to basic mutual misperceptions and generate hostility or alienation.

Goodwill and Intelligence Are Not Enough

Any American who promotes negative feelings and images in the minds of the hosts while he is in any foreign country is often assumed to be an ugly American in the sense that he has some defective personality traits that would be obvious to normal Americans. This is an unfortunate distortion of the real nature of cross-cultural interaction. Misunderstandings occur even if the guests are not especially insensitive or do not have malicious motives. Sometimes the conscious attempt to express goodwill rouses hostility. For example, a Chilean government official told me about a speech by Robert Kennedy that he witnessed in Santiago. The crowd's reaction was initially neutral but became hostile to the point where students were shouting, "Yankee go home," and throwing stones.

The phrase in the speech that triggered this inhospitable response was simply, "Let us learn together." Senator Kennedy had intended to convey an attitude of friendly equality to his audience. Unfortunately, this phrase has been used by North American officials on Latin American territory on several historical occasions, and that has given it a special meaning to Latin Americans according to the Chilean official:

> The phrase, "Let us learn together," would not have gotten this hostile response if the speaker had been Italian, Swedish, or Russian. They assume that when an American says it he is being a hypocrite because he is representing a government which has repeatedly taken advantage of Latin American countries through the use of both military, political and economic might. Often when the United States is about to put the pressure on us to do something they make it clear that we are working together.

This type of backlash produced by our good intentions happens not only occasionally to officials such as Richard Nixon, Robert Kennedy, and Nelson Rockefeller because of the historical context of United States–Latin American relations but also happens for nonhistorical reasons to the American guests in Colombian homes. Negative reactions were found to such well-meant acts as helping the maid with the dishes, taking the young children of the family to a movie, smiling at a receptionist, or waiting for a check to be cashed at the bank teller's window. Under certain circumstances, the guest's actions, motivated by goodwill, sometimes gave negative results when the intent was not accompanied with specific knowledge of the cultural pattern in which the actions were carried out.

Communication depends upon more than language. The facts throw serious doubt upon the assumption that if we can speak the foreign language fluently we can succeed in cross-cultural communication. It is not simply a matter of knowing the correct English translation for what is being said in Spanish. The reason that some conversations are meaningless to the American is *not* that the words have been translated incorrectly, but that the silent assumptions underlying the Colombian's words are different from those underlying the American's words. Each party to the cross-cultural conversation does not know that the other's words are based upon a different set of assumptions. In a sense, the words of each represent only part of the message that, added to the hidden assumptions, give the total message. Certain unspoken assumptions govern the interaction between people. The particular assumptions that are operative at a given moment are *situationally determined:* the operative assumptions are those that are culturally appropriate for people in certain roles who are interacting in a certain situation for some purpose.

Let us illustrate this general idea with a specific example. Two young

Spanish teachers from California had just arrived as house guests in a Mexican home. Lolita, the eight-year-old daughter in the family, was obviously very excited about the arrival of the guests who were to stay for several weeks. They were welcomed by Señora del Bosque, had been shown to their room, and were unpacking when the following conversation took place.

LOLITA. Mommie, let me go down with you to buy the meat for supper.
SEÑORA. Lolita, don't bother me, I'm busy right now!
(A few minutes later after all the guests had gotten unpacked.)
LOLITA. Mommie, let's go down to buy the meat for supper.
SEÑORA. I told you not to bother me, I'm very busy.
TEACHER A. Señora del Bosque, we are all moved in and were going to take a walk anyway, so why can't we go with Lolita to the market since you are so busy?
SEÑORA. No, thank you, the red flag is not out yet!
TEACHER A *(to teacher B)*. What does she mean "the red flag is not out yet"?
TEACHER B. Maybe she said *manera roja*, "the communist way," instead of *bandera roja*. Did you notice that faraway look in her eye? She was looking out the window while she was talking.
TEACHER A. I'm sure that isn't what she said because she has no reason to say anything about communists.
TEACHER B. But she doesn't want us to go with Lolita. That much is clear!

This case is typical in that when the words we hear don't seem to make sense, we tend to disbelieve our ears. But in this case the puzzling response, "No, thank you, the red flag is not out yet!" was correctly understood, and there is no other translation. Linguistically there is no lack of understanding because there is no single word that is not understood, and the syntax of the sentence does not provide any problem. Semantically, the meaning is clear in that for the North Americans the words have the same general referents as they do for the Latin Americans.

Then why did the North Americans puzzle over the meaning of this simple sentence? Because it did not seem to be an appropriate response to the teacher's question. It seems to be a non sequitur. It leaves the Americans confused as to what the señora expects of them. The response blocks their trend of activity without providing adequate explanation. What is the cause for this breakdown in communication? The response had no meaning to the Americans because they did not share the unspoken cultural context that was hidden in the señora's mind. The major premise needed to interpret the meaning of the response is only in the mind of the señora.

The North Americans did not understand one of the functions of a red flag in the foreign culture. In this particular situation, the meat market has no refrigeration, so the beef or pork may be brought directly from the slaughterhouse to the market where it is cut up and sold immediately before it can spoil. When the meat comes in the red flag goes out. This system is often used in small towns or in the small local neighborhood meat markets in the poorer sections of large cities. The assumption is that the customers in the neighborhood will keep a lookout for the red flag, buy the meat as soon as it comes in, take it home, and either refrigerate it or cook it immediately.

In this mini-drama the "faraway look" in the señora's eye was due to her focusing on the meat market a block down the street. Since she could see that the "red flag was not out yet," it made no sense to take Lolita to buy the meat. The North American's ignorance of this custom leaves a psychological vacuum which tends to be filled with some "explanation" more familiar to the American.

Trivial misunderstandings breed basic misconceptions. Often we tend simplistically to assume that misunderstandings over "trivial matters" would not lead to any serious consequences between people of intelligence and goodwill. Yet, we have considerable evidence that both the Americans and Colombians draw rather basic conclusions about the other's character as a result of "trivial" misinterpretations. In some cases the basic conclusion is created instantly, and in others it is the result of a gradual accumulation of misinterpretations.

It may seem "trivial" that the American guests, for example, did not make their own beds (it was not the maid's duty as they had assumed), did not dress appropriately, did not greet people properly, and didn't hang their bath towels out to dry in the sun; but these trivial acts were the result of miscommunication and the cause of further miscommunication and social isolation. Few Americans realized that such "trivia" led the majority of the Colombian hosts to conclude that their guests were "generally thoughtless of others," that "They think they are superior," and that "They do not care about their reputation among Colombians."

The Colombians had certain preconceptions and stereotypes of North Americans in general. Some of the stereotypes were positive and some were negative, some were reinforced by the direct acquaintance with the particular American guests, while others were counteracted. One of the positive stereotypes the Colombians seemed to have was of cleanliness. After all the United States is a land of automatic washing machines, abundant hot water, inexpensive soap, detergents, disposables, bathtubs, swimming pools, and deodorants. However, after making a more direct acquaintance with an American as a guest in his home, the Colombians began to change the stereotype to a negative one of the "dirty American."

Some specific dimensions of this image that were discovered and measured were: "They don't keep their rooms orderly"; "Their hair is not well groomed"; "They (males) do not clean their fingernails"; "They are disorderly in personal appearance"; "They do not bathe frequently enough"; and to top it off, "They smell bad at times."

When we traced the origin of the last two related images, we found that they were the result of a rather complex configuration of misunderstandings. The mere fact that the image of the American, in the mind of the Colombian who sees him every day, is negative does not tell us where the image is correct or incorrect. In the case of the "dirty American" image, the perception by the host was essentially correct. This does not mean, however, that the image is not the product of miscommunication. In this case the American's behavior itself was the result of miscommunication. Miscommunication contributed in two ways. Some Americans thought that in taking very few baths they were "doing as the Romans do"—they were trying to conform. A complex configuration of observations by the American contributed to his conclusion that the host family members rarely took baths. Other Americans took many fewer baths than they were accustomed to in the United States because they did *not* want to "do as the Romans do" (that is, what they *thought* the "Romans" were doing). Many thought that the host family usually bathed in cold water, a custom the guest was reluctant to imitate where the climate is chilly at 8,700 feet above sea level. Others misinterpreted the señora's remarks about their bathing in the evening as a criticism of using hot water for bathing.

Summary

Even intelligent and highly motivated students and Peace Corps trainees did not automatically learn how to behave as guests in a Colombian home merely by living there from three to nine months. Wide discrepancies are apparent between what the señora expected the guests to do and what the guests thought she expected of them. In some details, such as hanging one's towel in the sun each day, there was a *total* discrepancy between what the señora would have liked and what the guests thought she wanted. Similarly many guests did not know what their host considered permissible modes of dress in different times and places in the home. Many thought the maid made the bed; actually the disgruntled señora had been doing it for months. The guests tended to think of their own bedrooms as private and that they should not "invade" the señora's bedroom to watch television. Many guests discovered that bare feet were not considered permissible even in one's bedroom, but 38 percent of the guests never made this discovery. Of course we did not claim to find all of the things that the guests did not know or mistakenly thought they knew, but there is enough evidence to show that good intentions and intelligence are not enough to assure the discovery of even some of the simplest culture patterns which provide the context for daily interaction.

We cannot dismiss these gaps in communication as trivial simply because they are not dramatic, traumatic, or transcendental. We clearly demonstrated that many negative images and feelings are generated in the interaction between guests and hosts. It is of such "trivial" misunderstandings that general impressions are built. The host's negative judgments of the guest tend to isolate the American from the Colombian culture in which he is trying to immerse himself.

A vicious circle tends to operate. By observing the guest's behavior the host comes to conclusions regarding whether the American is the type of person he would like to have meet his friends and relatives, whether he is the type of person who would be "safe" to take to a party, a wedding, a picnic, a play, or a bullfight. If he feels that either he or the guest would not enjoy this experience, the host simply does not think of inviting the guest to such occasions. Thus, the host family unconsciously acts as a gatekeeper either to open a social door or leave it closed. When gateways to certain avenues of interaction are closed, the range of possible experience for the guests is reduced. In some cases the guest is given a trial run by being invited, for example, to a party; whether he is invited to another depends upon his behavior at the first. In other instances the guest never has the first chance because he has already given the impression that he would not enjoy it. Or, even though he might enjoy it, since he would make the Colombians uncomfortable, the host is unwilling to burden himself with a social liability. It was quite obvious in many cases that the host families considered the American guest as a social asset, especially those guests who had a high batting average in learning what was expected of them.

Since the major focus of this study is the nonlinguistic barriers to cross-cultural communication it is easy to give the impression inadvertently that either these particular Americans were insensitive and always projected a negative image or that these particular Colombians were prejudiced against their North American guests. Neither assumption is true. The Colombian hosts also had many positive images of their American guests.

Some of these images were consonant with stereotypes the Colombians already had and others were the result of direct observation of their particular guest and contrary to previously held stereotypes. Let us comment on each of the statements to supply some interpretive perspective.

"They rarely arrive late for an appointment." Punctuality was among the Colombians' stereotypes of North Americans, just as the lack of punctuality is among the North Americans' stereotypes of the Colombians. Usually punctuality was appreciated but upon certain occasions the American would arrive embarrassingly "early" for a Saturday night party. If it were announced for "about 8:30," he would arrive at 8:45 and be amazed to find the host was not at home yet. This caused uneasiness on both sides. However, the North American should not generalize from parties; business appointments are kept on time in Colombia. In general the Colombians thought of the Americans' punctuality as a good trait. A majority of 98 percent thought their American guests were punctual.

"They are generally people you can trust." It was our impression that Colombians *expected* North Americans to be both trusting and trustworthy and the Americans did nothing to damage this image while guests in the Colombian homes. A majority of 92 percent of the Colombian hosts felt their American guest was trustworthy.

"They do not always show off their money." Although there seemed to be a stereotype of the American as being rich, 81 percent of the Colombians seemed pleasantly surprised that they did not act that way.

"They study a lot when they are in Colombia." The image of studiousness was gained by the señora's direct observation of her guest who studied mainly in the bedroom.

"They introduce their friends when they should." The importance of introducing one's friends to the members of the family was stressed in the orientation of the Americans in all the programs placing them in Colombian homes. This willingness to introduce friends seemed to violate a stereotype of Americans.

"They do not tend to make promises they don't keep." Although 77 percent agreed with this positive image, some of the 23 percent who did not felt that the American sometimes failed to uphold his side of the implied promise in paying such things as taxi fare, theatre tickets, meal checks, and other sociability expenses.

"They do not try to give more advice than they should." The hosts seemed pleasantly surprised that the Americans did not give unsolicited advice. The hosts seemed to have had a stereotype of Americans coming to Colombia to "show them how things are done" in the United States.

"They bring gifts on occasions when they should." In spite of the guest's

good intentions he found it very difficult to know which occasions called for gifts. He succeeded enough to inspire a positive image, however.

"They are not anti-Catholic." The impression received from the interviews was that the señoras expected the North Americans to be "protesting" Protestants, and the majority were pleasantly surprised, just as many of the Americans were surprised that their host families were not proselytizing Catholics.

The above examples of positive images have been offered to show that relations between the host families and their guests were generally good, that neither the hosts nor the writer viewed the American students and Peace Corps trainees as peculiarly insensitive, unintelligent, or ill-willed. Their main problem was simply that they were Americans in a foreign culture. This needs to be said at the outset to put in better perspective the remainder of this book which concentrates on the problems, the miscommunications and the resulting *negative* images the hosts had of their American guests. Even though there were many positive images and feelings resulting from the interaction, it also became clear early in the research project that there were enough instances of miscommunication and resultant negative images to indicate that a detailed examination of the nature of the miscommunication would be extremely worthwhile.

The objective will be to describe and analyze the miscommunication that typically occurred between Colombian host families and their American guests. The description will be made from two different perspectives. Section I will describe the miscommunications according to the particular *scene* in which they take place; the four chapters in this Section deal with general household space, the bathroom, the bedroom, and the living room–dining room area. The kitchen is conspicuously absent because the American should not have entered the kitchen except on rare occasions. What little interaction there was in the kitchen appears in Section II in the chapter detailing the American's interaction with the maid.

In Section II the miscommunications will be described according to the role relationships involved—the problems arising in the general role of foreign guest, then the typical miscommunications associated with the guest's more specific relationship with the *señora*, the *señor*, the children, and the maid.

The final chapter is a summary of some of the practical and theoretical implications of these descriptions.

Fortunately, the American visitor in a foreign country does not have to understand all about the culture before he can communicate effectively. This is because much of the nonlinguistic content of the culture is situation-specific. Knowledge of a specific culture trait is necessary for effective communication only in certain situations and is irrelevant to communication in all other settings. For example, Colombians feel that the only appropriate place for the left hand at the dinner table is above the table, never in one's lap as is acceptable in the United States. Knowledge of this culture trait is necessary if the American guest is to understand the following conversation at the dinner table between the *señora* and her five year old child.

> MOTHER. Enrique, where is your hand?
> ENRIQUE (*bringing his left hand out from under the table*). Here it is, mamacita!
> MOTHER. That's a good boy!

The American's inability to understand the true social meaning of this exchange would be of little consequence if he merely concluded that he did not understand what was going on. Instead, in this case the American explained that "the mother was correcting Enrique for hiding his dirty hand under the table." This false conclusion was drawn from the combined evidence of the conversation plus the observation that Enrique's left hand was indeed dirty, which is not unusual for a five year old boy.

Similarly, an American student registering in a Latin American university cannot make sense out of many of the conversations between the Colombian students who share a basic knowledge of the institutional organization and the processes of matriculation. The American student unconsciously assumes many things about the matriculation process and setting that are not true. For example, he incorrectly assumes that there are certain days during which all students in the university must register regardless of their field of study, or that he has a choice of courses, or that once the class schedule is set it will not be changed one or more times during registration, or that he is free to take courses in several departments simultaneously, or that he will see a different set of students in his different classes during the week.

If the American doesn't realize that his assumptions are incorrect and if the Colombian student, professor, dean, or academic advisor is not aware of the vast gap between the American's silent assumptions and the institutional realities, any conversations between them can be confusing to both parties. Under these circumstances the best aid to communication for the American would be a clear explanation of how the Latin American university differs from the North American one. Then much of what the North American sees as "confusion, chaos, disorganization, and inefficiency" disappears.

The fact that specific bits of knowledge about a culture are necessary for face-to-face communication only in certain situations has a profound practical value. We know, for example, that certain communication problems are most likely to arise at a particular time and place in the daily routine of living in a Colombian home. Furthermore, if we know how foreigners from different nations vary in their expectations in a certain situation, we could predict, for example, that Americans would have communication problems in one situation while Italians would have problems in another even though they spoke equally fluent Spanish.

It is reassuring to know that a guest does not have to be prepared to deal with all possible communication problems at every moment. The sojourner in a foreign culture intuitively uses this principle by avoiding specific places, times, or topics where problematical communication is most likely to take place. The foreigner can concentrate his attention initially upon a few scenes in which he must participate for daily survival and then gradually branch out to other situations.

It is hoped that the following descriptions of the American guest trying to cope in different "scenes" in the Colombian household will provide some insight into the general principle that the interpretive context for any dialogue is contained in the social situation in which it takes place. When the scene changes there is a concomitant change in the potential activities, rules of the game, expectations, and assumptions that form the silent context used to interpret the true meaning of the verbal and non-verbal stimuli that are exchanged in each scene. The overt cues of place, time, props, and costume all help to remind the actors that certain subjective orientations are now appropriate and necessary for communication.

Every culture, like a play, has its script which requires certain persons to interact in specified ways at certain times and places, but also allows for some degree of ad libbing. When we are thrust into a foreign situation we often have the distinct sensation of being pushed onstage in the middle of an on-going play without a script, without knowing the roles of the other members of the cast, and with no inkling of the plot. In acute situations this can produce a state of near-panic.

Now let us turn to some of the scenes of miscommunication between the Colombian families and their American guests.

I

Scenes of Guest–Host Miscommunication in the Colombian Homes

2

Use of
Household Space

As a backdrop to the scenes of interaction inside the house we will give a broad view of the physical setting of the house in relationship to the neighborhood, particularly as it contrasts with the typical North American setting. Not all of these exterior physical differences are directly relevant to communication problems, yet an understanding of the external physical arrangements helps to clarify some aspects of the internal physical arrangements such as movement patterns, routes for entering or leaving the house, and certain feelings the Colombians have about interior zones of relative security from invasion of privacy or from robbery. Such factors in turn impinge upon the location of the maid's quarters, the family bedrooms, and the television set which are related to the kinds of silent assumptions made by Colombians regarding the functions of the interior space and the forms of behavior appropriate to different locations in the house. Finally, the differences between the North American's and the Colombian's silent assumptions regarding these different household scenes directly caused miscommunication between the Colombian host and the American guest.

General Physical Arrangements

In describing the common characteristics of the host families in Bogotá, which ranged from lower-middle to upper class, we do not pretend to generalize about homes in other regions of Colombia, particularly in the coastal lowland areas; nor can we assume that the homes of the *bogotano* lower class or the rural migrant population would be the same. We merely want to show the common patterns found among those host families in which the cross-cultural communication was studied. The commonly shared characteristics of the *bogotano* homes were the traits that differed most clearly from the typical middle-class urban home in the United States.

The front yards are much smaller than the back yards. Instead of having a sizable lawn area in front of the house, the houses are located much closer to the street than the North American would expect in an area of middle-class single-family residences. The front yards are small and contain a well manicured lawn and flowers. More of the land on a lot is walled in at the back of the house than is used for the front yard. This preference for more private space at the back can be clearly seen in the upper-class homes in the more luxurious residential areas where the lots may be three times as large as the average. The front yard is no larger, but the *patio* and *jardín* in back are.

Almost all of the host-family houses abut the houses of the neighbors on either side. In a typical residential block in the middle-class area, the facades of the abutting houses form a solid wall facing the sidewalk. There are no sideyards between houses permitting windows through which the neighbors could be observed. Neighbors cannot observe each other or chat over the side fence in the back yard because the rear patio and *jardín interior* are surrounded by a high wall. From the ground level one cannot observe the neighbors except those across the street. From the second floor the neighbors' houses abutting from behind can be seen as well as some portion of the patios and *jardines* of those on each side.

These two features clearly distinguish the spacial patterning of these *bogotano* houses from the homes of the North American guests who live there. Yet these two physical patterns may be two culturally different means to the same end of *privacy*. Privacy in the United States is obtained by increasing the open space between a person and his neighbor, while in Bogotá it is achieved by double abutting walls with no doors or windows.

The roofs, walls, and some of the floors are made of masonry, tile, or asbestos in a very high proportion of the houses. There are no combustible frame houses in middle-class Bogotá.

16

No back door gives access to the street or alley. There is an old Spanish saying that a house with two doors cannot be well guarded. All of the host family homes conform to this sentiment in having no back door giving access to the street. In the United States the back door to a home is an alternative route to the street or alley. None of the host-family homes and, indeed, none of the middle-class residential areas in Bogotá have an alley. The American becomes conscious of the importance of the concept of alley in his own culture by its absence in Bogotá. We have songs built on the alley theme such as "Alley Cat," "Sally in Our Alley," and many common colloquialisms involving the idea of alleys such as, "That's right down my alley"; these have no meaning in Bogotá.[1]

Since there are no alleys and since the houses have no space between them allowing a person to pass from the back yard to the street in front, the back door can go nowhere but to the back patio which is surrounded by a high wall. Sometimes the tops of these walls are bristling with jagged pieces of glass or with steel spikes to discourage thieves from climbing over or using the top of the wall as a catwalk from house to house.

More than 90 percent of the host houses have two floors. Most of the American guests came from middle-class homes that were one floor and perhaps had a basement. In contrast, nearly all of the host houses had a second floor, a few had a third floor, but none had a basement. The concept of the low, rambling, ground-hugging house surrounded by several thousand square feet of lawn to mow is a foreign image to the middle-class *bogotano*.

About two-thirds of the houses have some type of iron bars or ornamental grillwork over the downstairs windows. The American's reactions to the ironwork in the residential area is quite different from his reaction to the nonornamental riot screens that roll down to cover the first floor windows of many of the shops. The riot screens on the main thoroughfares are symbolic to the North American of looting and civil disorder. He tends to overreact to this sight.

The North American guest's reaction to the more aesthetic ornamental grillwork over the first floor windows in the residence is quite different. He often feels that it has more an aesthetic than a security function. It gives the windows an exotic, mysterious, romantic, lace-like effect that affords privacy and provides variety in the facades of the homes. The safety factor seems rather secondary to the North American as he talks about the grill-work. Some *bogotanos* say it is mainly for safety, otherwise the grillwork would also be on the second floor windows.

Over 95 percent of the host homes have special maids' quarters. That the maid is an integral part of the middle-class *bogotano* household is clearly expressed in the architecture of the house. The maid's quarters are nearly always located on the ground floor to give access to the service patio, kitchen, and garage without her having to pass through the dining room (*el comedor*) or living room (*la sala*) which are also on the ground floor. She has a room and private shower and toilet.

The location of her quarters is strategic for the maid's major functions. She is close to the kitchen where a large portion of her day is spent in dealing with the meals; she is close to the patio where she carries out another high priority function of washing the clothes by hand. (Only 22 percent of the host families had washing machines.) It is important to have *direct* access to the garage without passing through the living room and dining room areas of public *presentación* because the maid must frequently function as a receiver of deliveries made to the garage—wood for the fireplace (*leña*) which is delivered weekly on burroback, groceries, soft drinks, milk, and fruit juices which may arrive daily, and less frequently tanks of gas as well as receiving the repairmen and the gardener. The delivery men, even the milkman, won't leave anything on the doorstep but must directly hand the article to the occupant.

The maid's function as receiver of goods, although sporadically occupying only a small portion of her time, is essential to the smooth functioning of the household. It also frees the señora to leave the house to shop, work, socialize, go to Mass, or accompany the children to the school bus or playground. The *bogotano* middle-class family considers it imprudent to leave the house unattended at any time of the day or night.

The importance of the relationship between the architecture of the home and the status and functional relationships of its occupants is often brought home forcefully to the American wife who grows to like having a maid while living in Bogotá for a year or two. With the approach of her return to the United States she may toy with the idea of taking her maid, whom she has finally retrained into a more American pattern, back to the States with her. After some serious thought in trying to visualize the details of the maid's activities in the States, the wife realizes that the floor plan of the middle-class American house is not designed to keep the proper social distance between maid and the housewife or other members of the family. The maid is simply not built into the architecture of today's middle-class North American home.

The patio is located in the rear of the home. In the typical modern middle-class Bogotá residence the patio is not in the center of the house as it is in the older Colonial Period homes that followed the ancient Roman house pattern where the *peristylium* was in the center of the house surrounded by rooms on all four sides. Instead, more than 95 percent of the host-family homes have the patio in the rear of the house, sometimes bordered on one side by the maid's quarters. The area is divided into two parts. The *jardín interior* contains some combination of lawn, shrubs, flowers, and trees and is often directly accessible through the dining room or living room. The *patio de servicio* usually contains the facilities for washing and drying clothes, the tanks of pressurized gas used for cooking and heating water, housecleaning implements, and miscellaneous storage space. Where there is both a *jardín* and *patio*, the maid's quarters connect with the patio rather than with the *jardín*. Usually the kitchen has a door opening onto the patio.

Most host-family houses have garages that are an integral part of the house, but less than 50 percent of the families have an automobile. Although many American houses have a garage directly connected with the house, it is not an integral part of the house as it is in Bogotá.[2] For example, the United States garage is less clean and neat than the house. The American is more tolerant of oil spots on the floor of the garage; the *bogotano* has the maid scrub away all traces of oil from the tile floor. The interior finish of the American garage is usually not like that of the house; the interior of the *bogotano* garage often has ceramic tile walls and tile floors, and the garage door is often made of translucent glass overlaid with ornamental ironwork patterns matching those on the living-room windows which also face the street. There was not a single case among our sample of host families of the garage also doubling as a "do-it-yourself" shop with a work-bench and tools for household repairs or hobby. The middle-class husband simply does not act as a handyman around the house.

The kitchen, dining room, and living room are not clearly separated from the garage. In a few of the *bogotano* host homes there was only a low planter, banister, bookcase, or half-wall separating the garage from the house. The car, which was kept brightly polished, gave the impression to the American guest that it was on display.

> I went with Jorge to his cousin's house for a little party for a friend who was becoming a Jesuit priest. It really seemed peculiar. . . . There we were drinking Scotch and making toasts in this wall-to-wall white-carpeted living room with the car parked just five feet away with just a row of flowers in between. It sounds funnier in a way than it is . . . or at least funnier than it seems to me now that I'm used to it. But with carpet on one side of the room, a color-patterned tile floor on the other side where the car is, and just a planter in between sounds a little out-of-joint, but actually it looks nice . . . particularly when the car is polished so beautifully as it was that night.

In Bogotá a car, because of its high price, is more than a means of transportation. It is an instrument to reaffirm social status.

The North American's interpretation of the garage being spotless because it is a display room for the car may simply spring from his own cultural background in which the only place he has seen automobiles on polished floors is at the new car showroom where the cars are indeed on display. What he does not realize is that the garage has the additional function of providing party space for dances and play space for younger children. Therefore, by blending the garage into the living room a greater expanse is possible inside the house. This blending may be accomplished by simply eliminating all or part of the wall between the garage and the house proper.

Social Implications of the General Physical Arrangements

The idea that "a man's home is his castle" complete with the psychological moat and drawbridge seems to be more clear in the case of the host families than in the family backgrounds of the guests. This analogy can be carried further to say that the Colombian king of the castle is more free to roam outside the castle than his North American counterpart who is much more tied to his castle and to the queen.

The obstacles to exit by anyone but the father are shown in many ways. The American guests sense that the señora of the house is not so free to leave the house as the husband. She is not so free to go out at night without him, and she is more likely to have to account for her activities out of the house in the afternoon when she is most likely to leave the house. The husband rarely stays with the children to allow her to leave. Children, particularly daughters, must report precisely and faithfully where they are; the primary and secondary schools must assume more strict supervision in place of parents. Most of the private *colegios* (primary and secondary schools) pick up the children and return them very near their home. If no parent or maid is waiting at the bus stop, they may take the child back to school and call the parent rather than to leave a gap of a half block or a few moments with no one responsible. Children as old as 12 years often ride the *colegio* bus for a distance of two blocks because they are not allowed to walk that distance.

Young children in the middle class do not generally play in the streets or on the local neighborhood playground unless they are accompanied by a maid or other adult. This greater restriction to the home means there is much less involvement in team sports, more playing inside the home (in the patio, *jardín*, upstairs hall, or own bedroom), more gazing out of the upstairs windows as a pastime. Middle-class youngsters of elementary school age (whether boys or girls) do not have free access to the outdoors. Only the *gamines*,[3] who may or may not have legitimate parents but often have no home where they are welcome, play in the streets. Similarly, middle- or upper-class women do not have the same free access to the streets as those of the lower socioeconomic classes.

The lack of free access to the streets and movement in and out of neighbors' houses is accompanied by a strong impression by many North American guests that there is very little neighborliness.

> The families on our street just don't mix at all. I don't know why this is but it is not like in my parents' neighborhood in Detroit which is also a big city.

> My family doesn't seem to know any of the neighbors. I saw a Colombian girl about my age across the street and thought I would like to get acquainted with her so I asked the señora who lived there and she didn't know.

> There was a boy next door who was my age so I went over and talked with him. I was amazed when he said he had lived there for over a year because it was the first time I had seen him in the six months I had lived on the street.

Some North Americans speculate that this is partially caused by the physical arrangement of the houses on the block. The *bogotanos* do not agree with this. Their response is, "What would anyone be doing in the back yard? Only the maid and children ever use that area; we are not like North American parents who hang up the laundry, mow the lawn, plant a garden, and do many things in the back yard!" Sometimes they offer the explanation that the *bogotano* does not want to become involved with his neighbors just because of their physical proximity. If that is their only relationship, they will take advantage by "coming and borrowing things all the time" or "by sending their children over to play at your house so they won't dirty up their own house." This attitude is not very different from that found in the United States urban middle class.

One of the bases of neighborhood solidarity found in many United States cities—the overlap between the neighborhood and schools—is absent even in the suburbs of Bogotá. Most of the middle-class *bogotano* children attend private schools from kindergarten through the 11th grade. Children living on the same block may attend from five to 10 different *colegios*. In a United States middle-class residential area, the large majority of the children go to one public secular school, and all those living in a neighborhood who do not attend a public school probably attend one Catholic school. The school provides a common experience, a common background, for all the children in a neighborhood and also builds up peer-group relationships that carry over between neighborhood and school. Parents often get acquainted with neighborhood families whose children play with their own. Also, many middle-class public schools in the United States have a fairly active PTA, which means that some of the

21

parents in a neighborhood get acquainted with each other as fellow members of the PTA.

In Bogotá the lack of carryover between children's peer groups at school and in the neighborhood is further emphasized by the fact that the length of the school day leaves little time for play. Typically, a child leaves home in the morning at 7:30 or 8:00 to catch the bus to school. He may come home for lunch on the same bus, but there is no time to play. He returns from school anywhere between 4:45 and 6:00 depending on the school and whether he is at the beginning or end of the bus run. It is dark between 6:00 and 6:30.

The lack of correspondence between neighborhood and school is an inhibiting factor that would have to be overcome if Bogotá were to have the same amount of interaction between neighbors as a United States city of comparable size.

Another recurring theme in the North Americans' observations is that a much larger proportion of the visitors in the Colombian home are relatives. Typically, since many of the host families are those whose children have married and left, there is a lot of visiting from the married sons and particularly daughters who come with their new families on the weekends to visit. The residential propinquity of all the members of an extended family in Bogotá, Bombay, or Bagdad would be greater than in Denver, Detroit, or Danville. There are several reasons for this. First, in the more agrarian-based economies, the few large cities contain a much larger portion of the total country's population than in the United States. Second, this population is more concentrated so that the travel distances within the metropolitan area are less than in the industrial-based city. Third, the migration pattern in the agrarian-based economy is one in which the younger people migrate into, rarely out of, the large city. There is very little migration of the middle-class population from one large city to another in contrast to the United States. This means that in Bogotá there is a much greater tendency for those who come to the city from smaller cities, towns, and villages to stay. Their children and grand-children also stay.

That the house is more open to kinfolk and less open to fellow workers, colleagues, or neighbors is shown in many small ways. For example, the host families are much less likely to give the new guest "the grand tour" of the house to show him every nook and corner. Many Colombian professors who are well acquainted and teach in the same field at the same university for years have never been inside each other's homes even though they may live nearby.

In short, the house is more strictly a family thing in the sense of a tendency to exclude nonrelatives and to include relatives beyond the nuclear family. This tendency is not necessarily correlated with a strong equalitarian "togetherness" within the nuclear family of husband, wife, and children.

Use of Upstairs versus Downstairs Areas

In Colombia, there is a real difference in the way various activities are distributed between the upstairs and downstairs areas. The cultural difference in the *use* of household space is greater than the differences in the *physical appearance* of comparable rooms in the U.S. and Colombian households involved. The host-family upstairs is physically more like the upstairs in an American home than the downstairs. However, the actual function of the upstairs hall and the bedroom differs from the North American home.

A much greater portion of the family's time is spent upstairs in the hall and bedroom areas than an American family's. The guests who were interviewed showed surprise in most cases that the family spent so little time downstairs.

> Visitors always, or just about always, visit upstairs in the bedroom. The lady of the house talks in secret with her sister in her bedroom and I think they feel safe talking on the phone upstairs.

> Much more of the time is spent upstairs than downstairs. Leisure time is spent by the señora in her bedroom. The downstairs is used only by the children to play, for meals, and for guests.

> The family lives upstairs most of the time. They never use the living room which is downstairs but use the upstairs hall to congregate.

> We sometimes go upstairs after *la comida* (dinner) to look at T.V. or something. In two months the downstairs living room has been used only two times at night.

> The family prefers to gather in the evening in the parents' bedroom where the television is.

> Even the local parish priest came to see the señora and visited with her in the bedroom. I realized later that was perfectly normal, at least for any friends who come to visit.

The American guest is impressed by this unfamiliar behavior pattern. Usually, he first assumes that this is a pattern peculiar to his particular host family but sometimes discovers in conversations with guests from other homes that this is a general cultural pattern.

The Colombian señora is not so tied to the kitchen as the North American wife. The fact that the maid cooks, washes dishes, sets and clears the table makes it possible for the housewife to escape the kitchen area. She has no need to develop ways to be sociable with adult friends or to supervise young children's play while working in the kitchen. The American floor plan in which the kitchen, dining area, or living room area are mingled rather than being formally separated rooms was never found in any of the host-family houses. Some did mingle the dining area and the living room.

The señora can more easily avoid interruption if she stays upstairs. Since many of the families have only one maid and the señora must share some of the work, there is the tendency for the señora to do most of the daily upstairs chores and leave the cooking, washing, and ironing to the maid. Since the maid is downstairs, she can also answer the door and receive deliveries so the señora will not be interrupted so often.

The upstairs provides more privacy for the señora. In view of the upstairs–downstairs division of labor with the maid, the señora would prefer to do her telephoning, a favorite indoor sport, from upstairs where the maid is less likely to overhear the conversation and where she can be dressed less formally than would be required if she were in the living room. All of the host families had a telephone, and more than 70 percent were located upstairs either in the hall or in the señora's bedroom. In many cases there were jacks to plug in a telephone downstairs as well as in the upstairs hall and the master bedroom.

The señora might feel more secure upstairs. Several types of remarks spontaneously offered in sociable conversations and elicited in formal interviews suggested the security factor as a real one.

> They are afraid to have anyone sleep downstairs. It was robbed very recently.

> We were upstairs and heard this noise in the dining room at 3 o'clock in the afternoon. The señora called down to Rosa, the maid, to ask what had happened. The maid didn't answer so she went down to find that she had just been robbed of the silverware, and the maid was afraid to scream or shout while the robber was there.

> When we went away on vacation our maid refused to sleep downstairs in her room unless her sister could come to stay with her. Since this was inconvenient I suggested that she sleep upstairs in the front bedroom the week we were away. She was glad to do that.

> The grandmother in my host family who is always worried about security since the Bogotazo in 1948 spends all her time upstairs.

Against this somewhat impressionistic background of the general indoors–outdoors and upstairs–downstairs activity patterns, we will now supply more detailed description of the differences in activity patterns in specific rooms.

Notes

1. In Spanish the words *callejuela* or *callejón* which are usually given in Spanish-English dictionaries as meaning *alley* rarely refer to a passageway behind a row of houses. Some Latin American tourist departments unfortunately translate the word *callejón* to alley in English. For example, the tourist literature on the picturesque colonial style city of Guanajuato in Mexico translates the *Callejón del Beso* into "The Alley of the Kiss." To the North American *alley* connotes the seamy side of the residential area with the garbage cans, hence the rats, hence the cats—a far cry from the romantic street so narrow that lovers may kiss across the street from the balconies above. Actually this *Callejón del Beso* is a picturesque, romantic, narrow, crooked street because the houses face it on both sides.

2. The difference between the North American and Latin American attitude toward the garage might possibly have historical roots in the former traditional locations of the shelter for the carriage. As shown in the architecture of many of the old colonial houses in Latin America, a large entrance was provided to allow the carriage into the central patio of the house. On the North American scene the carriage and the stable were outside and separate from the house or inn. In the private dwellings there were no walls holding the carriage house, stables, and living quarters within one unit. Today, in the old colonial period homes in Mexico and Colombia, it is not uncommon to take advantage of the carriage entrance to keep the car in the central patio.

3. Crude estimates of the number of *gamines* range from three to five thousand in Bogotá. José Gutiérrez, *Infancia de la Miseria* (Bogotá, Biblioteca de Bolsillo, 1967), p. 9.

3

The Bathroom

The bathroom was the object of most of the conflict and confusion between hosts and guests. Even in the homes that had a private bath for the guest many sources of miscommunication centered around its use.

All of the host homes had at least one bathroom upstairs, and half had an additional small guest bathroom (*el baño de emergencia*) downstairs, which was nearly always off the living room, hall, or foyer. Fifty percent of the homes had two bathrooms upstairs.

Upstairs bathrooms have toilet and shower. The shower may be a large three- by six-foot or smaller stall with a curtain. Typically, the shower in the maid's quarters and in *el baño de emergencia* is only a shower head above a grilled drain in the tile floor located in the small space between the toilet bowl and the lavatory. It is difficult to shower and keep the toilet paper, towels, or anything else in the room dry.

In contrast to the North American middle-class bathroom, only 16 percent of the host-family bathrooms had a bathtub. This is not necessarily an indication of the high cost of bathtubs but is part of a deeper cultural aversion to bathing (or washing dishes or clothes) in standing rather than running water.

Bogotanos pointed out that families tend to be larger than in the United States and since it is customary to bathe at least once a day, it is simply too time consuming to have to fill the tub, drain the tub, and clean it before reuse. The bathtub is thought of as a rather dirty thing, impractical with large families, and certainly not worth the cost.

Many maids did not put water in the sink or dishpan when washing dishes. Instead, they kept the water running; scraped the dish; washed it with a soapy brush, sponge, or cloth; and then rinsed it under the same running faucet.

Bogotanos assume dishes are washed in cold rather than hot water, and it is much cheaper to do so. One señora said, "Can you imagine doing dishes in a pan of cold water?" It would leave a messy conglomeration of grease and soap curds. In her mind the emphasis was on *pan*, while for the North American listener, the emphasis was on *cold*; but both would agree that if cold water is used, it would be better to use running water. Some señoras complained that if any hot water was left in the tank when it was time to wash dishes, the maids would quickly use it all by leaving the faucet running while they made frequent trips to the refrigerator or dining room table; the dishes would still be washed in cold water.

North American guests often found it difficult to buy stoppers (*tapones*) for bathroom lavatories and sinks, which added credence to their idea that the Colombians don't want to wash anything in standing water if it can be avoided.

The lack of stoppers encountered by the North American has another interesting explanation by Colombians who point out that the North American should not expect to find a sink stopper in a store that sells sinks.[1] Stoppers might be available in a variety store such as *Ley* or *Tía*, but items are often unavailable for extended periods of time because of problems in the retail distribution system.

The preference for showers instead of bathtubs, washing dishes in running water, and the lack of stoppers all seemed to some North Americans as manifestation of a cultural preference for using running water. Actually, when seen from the Colombian point of view the pattern cannot be explained that simply. Often the outsider has an oversimplified "explanation" for cultural patterns.

Another clear difference between the American and the *bogotano* bathroom is in the presence of the bidet (*bidé*). Over 60 percent of the host-family bathrooms had a bidet, which was an exotic fixture to many of the American guests. This bit of European civilization is a welcome aid to personal hygiene in Colombia but is very rare in the United States. During the first few weeks of the American guests' stay, jokes often circulate about some guest who was trying to discover the function of the gadget and turned a combination of valves which won him a squirt in the face.

Misperception and Confusions

The North American guest quickly becomes accustomed to the physical differences in the bathroom but takes longer to discover the different pattern of its use. There is no uniform pattern for all the host families, but many of the families follow patterns that are strange to most of the North American guests. Confusions and misperceptions result for the guests and the host families.

Proper dress

One of the persistent complaints from a significant minority of the host families is that the North American guest runs about the house in an unacceptable state of dress or undress. One occasion is often when the *norteamericano* is on the way to the bathroom in the morning.

> One of the *gringas* always went to and from the bathroom in just her pants and bra, which my own daughters never did.
>
> Barbara would always go to the bathroom in her "babydoll" pajamas. I told her not to but she kept going in her "babydolls."
>
> The first girl I had would go naked from the bathroom to her bedroom with the clothes she had taken off in her hands. Many times there were people visiting in the upstairs hall, and I considered that very bad.
>
> He doesn't wear a pajama top and has only one pajama bottom, which he has sent to be washed only one time in almost two months. He shouldn't walk down the hall this way.
>
> Roberto didn't bring a bathrobe, pajamas, or slippers. He'd sleep in shorts and just put on his trousers to go to the bathroom. I didn't like this.
>
> I guess there is nothing really wrong with walking down the hall barefooted, but it might be harmful for his health.

Probably most of the North American guests came to realize that such behavior could be quite shocking to the Colombian family. But many never discovered that behavior much more conservative than these examples was also considered inappropriate for a well-behaved guest.

Señoras told the Colombian interviewers what form of dress they considered proper for their guests when going from their bedroom to the bathroom in the morning. North American guests told North American interviewers what they thought their señora perceived to be the proper dress for this occasion. The degree to which American guests misperceived their señoras' expectations can be used as an indicator of the communication gap between the host and guest. This gap between how the host expected the guest to behave and what the guest thought the host expected is particularly significant in view of the fact this lack of communication involved *daily* activities in the household and the American guests had been living in the home from about 12 weeks to 24 weeks depending upon the type of training program in which they were involved.

The greatest communication gap for the female guests was the appropriateness of wearing a "slip, bra, and pants only" on the way to the bathroom. After several months in the homes 31 percent of the guests incorrectly thought that their señora felt this to be an appropriate form of dress. The next largest communication gap was in regard to going barefoot on the morning trek to the bathroom. About 26 percent of the North American female guests incorrectly thought that the señora would approve of this.

For the male guests the biggest communication gap in this setting is with respect to the appropriateness of wearing all three articles—pajamas, bathrobe and slippers—to the bathroom. While *all* of the hosts thought this most appropriate, only 50 percent of the guests felt it would be perceived as appropriate by the host. Generally, in the case of the more modest forms of dress fewer guests than hosts thought them appropriate, but in the case of the less modest modes of dress (barefoot, pants and slippers only, and underwear only) more guests than hosts thought them appropriate.

The Colombian señora's standards of modesty seem to be more strict for the female than for the male guest. For example, 29 percent of the hosts approve of the male going barefooted, but only 20 percent approve for the female guest. It is abundantly clear that all of the señoras would approve of the wearing of pajamas, slippers, and bathrobe by both the male and female guests.

In addition, dress had to be more modest or conservative if people of the opposite sex from the guest were at home at the time, or if there were other guests of either sex in the home at the time, or if the *norteamericano* were not going to the bathroom specifically to bathe.

In deciding whether wearing pajamas without a bathrobe was permissible, the señoras would point out that if the pajamas were heavy (not sheer) or if the bathrobe were heavy and opaque (rather than a sheer dressing gown) they would be more acceptable.

Sharing the bathroom

Some of the families complained that the *norteamericano* spent excessive amounts of time in the bathroom. As one Colombian put it:

Oh yes, he stayed in the bathroom as if he were a woman. It would take a long time for him, and if my husband didn't get up at five o'clock in the morning, he would be late for the office. That's the problem in my house.

My husband says, "no more students" because I have to get up very early to find the bathroom empty. We have an emergency bath, but the students don't think that they could use that one, so my husband and my son had to use the emergency bath.

In some cases the North American guest had not the faintest notion that he was depriving others of access to the bathroom. As one student said:

They have never mentioned any problem in getting to the bathroom because I'm in there. Most of the family uses it very early before I get up. If they needed to get in, they could certainly just knock or say something.

Some families consider it impolite to knock when someone is in the bathroom with the door closed. One señora was obviously indignant with the North American guest who did knock on the closed bathroom door:

If I were in the bathroom, she would beat on the door. She was very badly brought up. She should have just gone down to the emergency bathroom.

Some of the North Americans thought that a member of the Colombian family would feel free to let them know that he was waiting for the bathroom, and they did not feel bad about spending time there. Sometimes a *norteamericana* would be washing her underwear or the *norteamericano* would be shaving with an electric razor. The girl should not be washing in the bathroom in the morning when most of the family tries to take a bath, and the electric shaver could just as well be used in the guest's own bedroom without using the bathroom. In either case the door could have been left open to permit communication.

The problem of the North American's blocking access to the bathroom without realizing it is compounded by the fact that he would like to spend more time in the bathroom when living in a foreign culture than he would at home. It is one of the very few places he finds privacy, and he often feels a great need for privacy to retreat temporarily from the psychological stresses and strains of the cross-cultural encounter.

The North American guest also complained that often he could not get into the bathroom when he wanted to, especially in the mornings. Sometimes he was needlessly exasperated because he had not yet acquired the habit of thinking of the *baño de emergencia* downstairs. In other cases he wanted his toothbrush, shaving equipment, shampoo, or other toilet articles which, according to his own cultural pattern, he left in the upstairs bathroom. This inconvenience could have been avoided if he had followed the more typically Colombian pattern of keeping towel and toilet articles in his own room.

Personal toilet articles

A majority of the señoras (59 percent) expect the North American guest to keep his towel and toilet articles in his own room, but only 30 percent of the American guests realized this expectation after living in the home for several months. This minority of Americans would have been even smaller if they had depended upon their own observations or communication with the host family for the discovery. North Americans who made the discovery passed it along to others.

The señoras who felt it would be proper for their guest to keep towels and toilet articles in the bathroom had a separate bath for the exclusive use of the guest or two bathrooms upstairs, one of which was assigned to the guest and a child of the same sex and age. Some señoras had their own separate bath connected to the master bedroom and never shared it with the guest. Some of the señoras pointed out that when there are young children using a bathroom none of the adults should leave their towels in the bathroom because the children will get them dirty quickly.

One reason towels are not left in the bathroom in Bogotá is that they will not dry there. The climatic conditions present a basic problem of getting the towels dry if one bathes every day. The amount of moisture to be absorbed by a bath towel can be reduced by more than half by taking a few moments to rub off much of the water by hand before using the towel.

About 60 percent of the señoras expected the guest himself to hang his towel in the service patio to dry each day. It is interesting to note that *not a single North American guest* who was interviewed knew that the señora expected the towel to be hung out each day.

The degree to which a towel or a bar of soap is considered a *personal* item also caused misunderstandings. Most of the señoras felt the guest should furnish his own, but not many guests realized that this was expected. The cross-cultural difference in attitude toward soap is found even outside the household in hotels and public rest rooms. For example, I recently traveled through many of the cities of South America, staying in typical Latin American hotels. I discovered that they furnish towels, but the soap was always "missing." When the bellboy was asked to bring soap, he went out to buy it and presented a special bill for it, just as if he had been asked to bring a cigar. This suggests that the bar of soap is considered a personal item or that it is relatively more expensive than in the United States.

31

The *bogotano* families who did not expect the guest to furnish his own bath towel and soap were generally in the upper-income range of the middle class.

"That dirty communal towel"

Several of the guests complained that in the bathroom there was only one "communal towel" which was so dirty that they didn't like to dry their hands on it, much less their faces. They had assumed that it was communal in the sense that the guest was also expected to use it. This was *never* the case; he was expected to have his own towel. Usually, the towel in the bathroom was used only by the children, who have a tendency to soil towels unnecessarily.

How often is bathtime?

If the guest is to minimize problems arising from competition for the bathroom, he must understand the typical bath schedule of the host families. Among host families the norm regarding the frequency of bathing can be simply stated: "Everyone should bathe at least once a day." Unfortunately, this norm is not communicated to many of the North American guests! Almost all of the señoras expected their guests to take a bath at least once a day, while only about half of the guests thought this was expected of them. An even more dramatic contrast was found in that *all* of the señoras recognized that there are times when the guest should take a bath *more* than once in the same day, but *none* of the North American guests thought the señora could expect such a thing.

When is bathtime?

If the North American guest is going to live up to the Colombian's (or his own) standards of taking the daily bath, it is helpful for him to understand when the most convenient time for him to take a bath would be. Many of the North American guests thought they should shower in the morning because that is when the members of the host family bathed. But if we consider the possible competition for bathroom during this peak-load time, we can understand why some of the señoras recommended the evening bath for the guest. When there were two or more bathrooms the señoras felt that the morning bath was best for several reasons. The clearly salient were that the hot water heater was routinely lit early in the morning specifically for bathing and was turned off after breakfast, and the maid or the señora wanted to have the bathroom cleaned only once each day after everyone had taken baths. The señora's friends rarely visit in the morning, but things must be neat for visitors in the afternoon.

One reason some of the North Americans felt they should take their bath in the morning, even though it was obvious that this increased the competition for bathroom time, was that they noticed that the hot water heater was never lit in the evening, and they didn't want to take a cold shower. The majority of the señoras thought the guest should ask the maid to light the water heater any time he wanted to take a bath, but less than one-fourth of the North American guests thought this to be the case. The other señoras either thought the guest should ask them to light it or have the guest light it himself. A few of the señoras said that in their homes there was hot water all the time and the heater was never turned off. The main purpose of turning off the water heater after bathtime is to save expensive gas. Most of the water heaters have thermostats, but the cost of maintaining the temperature at the proper level from one bathtime to the next is assumed to cost considerably more than turning it off and heating it again later.

Leaving the bathroom dry and tidy

Colombians appeared to their American guests to have an excessive concern over the appearance of their floors, so when having a wet bathroom floor contributed to making the other floors messy, the problem was multiplied. One of the common complaints of the señoras was that the guest left the bathroom floor too wet. Since the floor was invariably tile, the American did not feel that this should be particularly objectionable, but to the señora it was very important.

> When she took a shower, she must have left the curtain open because the floor was splashed and wet.
>
> The floor was so wet in the bathroom that when anyone came out the rest of the morning they tracked up the polished floor in the upstairs hallway.
>
> When the floor was so wet, people would come in and leave black footprints on the bathroom floor and the maid or I would have to mop it again.

When the host wanted to pay a great compliment to the tidiness of the guest, she would tell how he left the bathroom in perfect condition.

Some of the American guests became aware of what they called "the señoras' obsession with neatness," but they showed little awareness of the connection between a wet floor in the bathroom and the footprints in the hall. Also, they assumed that the maid would clean it up and that she was an *additional* convenience in the house that they didn't have in the States. They did not seem to realize that buying groceries, cooking, cleaning, washing, and ironing takes more time than in the United States where there are many more electrical appliances in the household. It was not uncommon for some of the American guests to express a feeling that the maid was overworked while at the same time adding to her load.

Using a washcloth

Washcloths are not commonly used in the Colombian home. Some of the señoras thought of the use of the *toallita* as a dirty habit.

> She always left her *toallita* hanging in the bathroom and it gets smelly if it doesn't dry for a few days, and when it does get dry it is stiff with dirt.

> He tells me that he uses the *toallita* to wash himself all over when he takes a shower, but why wash with that dirty thing when you have soap and clean water?

> The *toallita* is a good place for germs to hide unless you wash it after each time you use it. I understand that they are beginning to sell them here in Bogotá, but I wouldn't own one myself.

In general, the American guests who used washcloths in bathing were looked upon with curiosity or thought of as using an unsanitary method of bathing. Some of the American guests began to agree with the Colombians before the end of their stay and threw the washcloth away.

Bathroom Patterns and Cross-cultural Communication

The seemingly trivial differences in the cultural patterns of bathroom use were found to be serious stumbling blocks to communication. In many cases the misunderstandings influenced a sizable minority of the Colombian hosts to conclude that it was part of the North American national character to be "dirty" and "untidy." It is of such stuff that international images are built, so it becomes difficult to dismiss the cross-cultural differences in bathroom behavior as mere trivia.

The Colombians and North Americans had a *reciprocal* view of each other as being dirty. This image was not simply a stereotype or prejudgment but was based on direct observation of each other's behavior. Part of the North Americans' reputation for being dirty was due to cultural differences as to where and how the virtue of cleanliness is practiced, and part of this image was due to the fact that the North Americans could not overcome those communication barriers necessary to live up to their own standards of bodily cleanliness under the strange conditions in which they found themselves. Much of the confusion for the North American guest was due to his lack of understanding of some of the physical and social patterns of the host-family bathroom.

The Colombians' image of the dirty norteamericano

The unflattering image of dirty North Americans was pervasive. It seemed to be a product of the face-to-face communication between North Americans and Colombians, since this image was *not* part of the stereotype Colombians have of North Americans.

Needless to say, this image came as a surprise to the North American guests themselves, which is another indication of the lack of communication between the Colombian host and the North American guest. It is perfectly understandable that most people would be reluctant to tell a person who is not only a guest in their home but also a foreigner that they "shouldn't be so dirty." Colombians interviewed the señoras to discover how prevalent this image was and to obtain some clues regarding the concrete bases for the image, the assumptions involved, and some clues as to why in those rare cases where the señora tried to correct the North American's behavior, she was usually unsuccessful.

A sizable minority agreed with four statements regarding the personal cleanliness of the North American guests. In response to the questionnaire, 37 percent agreed that "They are disorderly in personal appearance"; 42 percent agreed that "They don't keep their hair well groomed"; 39 percent agreed that "They don't bathe frequently"; 27 percent agreed that "They smell bad at times."

To gain some insight into the possible problems of interpreting this information to North Americans, we obtained the reaction of various students and professors in the United States. The most striking aspect of these spontaneous responses was what might be called the legitimation-by-majority-vote expressed in such observations as the following:

> But in general the Colombians didn't agree that they were actually "dirty" Americans.

> The only place where the Americans didn't get a majority rejecting the negative image is in the case of the hair.

> I'm happy that only 27 per cent of the Colombian hosts thought that their American guest "smelled bad at times."

Those who didn't seem to be very impressed with the minority agreement with the negative images seemed to assume that as long as the majority were perceived in positive terms we have "won the battle." Such reactions did not represent the majority who fortunately realized that if Americans are interested in the image they project, in the willingness of the Colombian family to take another American guest, or in not having Americans excluded from social situations by Colombians, Americans should be interested in reducing these negative images toward the zero point.

The most prevalent theme in the open-ended statements of the señoras was that the American was dirty *because* he did not bathe frequently enough.

The problem with these girls is their untidiness and lack of cleanliness . . . after having two girls I have decided not to have any more in my home.

If she took her shoes off, we could smell her feet. It got to be embarrassing because it got beyond the hiding stage and my children began to make remarks.

She did not take a bath very often but she did look clean and would change her clothes often.

He didn't have a bath very often even though I would tell him there was hot water.

I was very shocked because they didn't take a bath every day, but they did leave the bathroom clean.

They didn't have a bath very often and they say that the Colombians are the ones that don't bathe very often.

He looked dirty because he very seldom had a bath. In six months that he was with us, he had five or six baths, and because of this his comb was always very dirty.

He was tidy in the use of the bathroom but he didn't bathe often.

I told her that she had no right to keep her feet that way and that she should get some pumice stone and wash them well. None of the girls I had bathed daily.

Sometimes she smelled bad and I think she didn't bathe often enough because she smelled bad, especially at times. When she came into the room, you'd notice it and that's very bad. I could not say anything to her because that is very difficult.

He didn't bathe every day. He was clean in the fact that he changed clothes every day and he looked very clean, but he had a bath only once a week.

They did not have a bath every day. At the beginning we thought they were going to be very clean because the first day they had two baths. Maybe they were tired and wanted a bath to rest, but then they would have a bath every third or fourth day.

Reasons for avoiding the bath. Interviews with the American guests showed that the Colombians' image of them as nonbathers was essentially correct in that most Americans admitted that they took many fewer baths in Bogotá than was their custom in the United States. Although there were several distinctly different reasons why different Americans avoided the bath, most of the reasons directly or indirectly were based upon miscommunication and misinterpretation of their own observations in the home.

First were those Americans who honestly thought they were "doing as the Romans do" by taking fewer baths than they would like. They believed that the Colombians simply had lower standards of bodily cleanliness than did North Americans as shown in the following excerpt.

Let's face it, if things were the same here as in the United States, there would be no reason to come. Some of the kids complain that they can't get a bath as often as they like, but what can they expect! Hot water costs money where you have to use bottle gas. Also, you have to admit that most of these Colombian homes where we live are cleaner than Colombia in general. Once you get used to the sight of men urinating in public and take a look at the market with the flies all over the food and get used to the idea that you will never find any toilet paper in a public toilet, things don't look so bad in your Colombian home. They are just not so obsessed with the idea of cleanliness as we are. You know that when you see the dirty communal towel in their bathroom. Also, you can certainly see it in the kitchens—not just in my house but in those of some of my American and Colombian friends. It is about the same everywhere. The stove is dirty and greasy. There is grease on the wall and ceiling near the stove. The thermostat on the water heater is so coated with grease that it probably doesn't work. The water heater flue on it to take the fumes outside just goes out into the kitchen. There are no screens on the windows to keep the flies out. Some of the girls tell me that the dishes are never really clean because they are washed in cold water by the maid. And a lot of the maids do not look very appetizing to me. They just don't look clean. It's no wonder that they don't want anybody but the maid in the kitchen. Everybody I talk to finds another interesting thing; there are very few wastebaskets in the house, which makes it a bit hard to keep things as tidy as you'd like. We have to be a bit flexible and adjust to these things. After all, this is not the richest country in the world. I figure that if I get one or two baths a week, that's not bad. A lot of people in the States don't do any better. Some of the people in our city slums don't even have a bath or shower in their home but have to go to public baths. So why can't we be a good sport about this instead of being those "superior and demanding *gringos*" the Colombians don't like.

This type of North American guest is doing his best to adjust cheerfully to what he believes to be the Colombian norm of bathing infrequently. The thought that the Colombians do not bathe frequently is not a result of direct observation of their bathing habits. Instead, it is a conclusion based upon the unconscious assumption that people in a particular culture are either clean or dirty and that, if they have unsanitary practices in one area, they will be unsanitary in another.

The important point here is that this well-meaning person is adapting his behavior to what he believes to be the norm of personal bodily cleanliness in Colombia. He indirectly deduces this norm from his basic assumption that cleanliness is a national character trait (which, if present, will be manifested in all realms of life) plus his observation of certain unsanitary practices that impress him because they are foreign. This operation of global overgeneralization raises three interesting questions: Why has he not noticed that this assumption is not true in his own culture? Why didn't he generalize from those specific areas in which the Colombians are more clean than the North Americans? Why has he not observed that Colombians take a daily bath in the host family where he has been living several months?

Two considerations help answer the first question. First, this assumption is often completely unconscious and therefore never subjected to any rational scrutiny. Second, even though he may be aware of certain areas of cleanliness and uncleanliness in his own culture, the person may still assume that the *same pattern* of cleanliness is found in all cultures that hold cleanliness to be a virtue.

The second question is particularly fascinating since in many areas of neatness, tidiness, or cleanliness, the North American guests do not attain the standards of the host household. Possibly the visible items of cleanliness are not used as a basis for concluding that the norms of bodily cleanliness are also high because when one judges a different cultural pattern according to his own cultural premises, he is much more aware of the differences that violate his own sensitivities and give rise to a strong feeling of revulsion or frustration. The areas in which higher standards are exercised often cause no discomfort to the foreigner and therefore may not often be noticed. When these exist, instead of reacting positively, the foreign visitor often gives them a negative connotation because this is considered "overdoing a good thing." This point is illustrated by statements extracted from interviews with North Americans.

> The Colombians have what I call the "cult of the floor." They ritualistically clean the floor several times a day in public buildings and several times a week in private homes. Meanwhile they are neglecting many more important types of cleanliness and sanitation.
>
> My family is a little bit nutty on keeping everything neat. The maid always straightens up my desk in my room. They hide the newspaper on Sunday so that it won't be cluttering up the *salón*, and they won't let kids play with any toys downstairs because it may not be perfectly presentable if company comes.
>
> It's funny how they keep the car all "spit and polished" and the garage without a speck of dirt, but the milk is not pasteurized and the druggist at the local *inyectoria* wipes the hypodermic needle off on his white coat before giving you a shot.

The basic implication of such statements is simply that the Colombian is acting in an irrational manner, such as compulsiveness or some other form of irrationality; therefore, the explanation is assumed to be a *national* character trait.

A North American guest may not discover the bathing pattern of the host family where he has lived for several months because he is often not home or awake when members of the family are bathing. Typically, the father in the family rises early, takes a bath, eats breakfast and leaves about 7:30 a.m. He takes a shower quickly and leaves the bathroom without a trace of a shower having been taken. The señora may take a bath later in the morning after the North American student has left the house.

A second type of North American guest simply took advantage of the absence of the social pressures that operate on him in the United States. The physical education program strongly affects many of the students' bathing schedules at their colleges where, for example, all the members of the gym class shower before going back to classes. In Bogotá there is very little occasion for sports and no showers outside the private home except for private clubs where students are usually not eligible. Also, the Colombian señora rarely feels free to exert any pressure on the North American guest to take a bath.

> I know that some of the students have not come up to the once-a-week standard of bathing because no one pushes them.

> The Colombian custom of bathing every day prevails, but the señora doesn't force it on me in any way.

> She (the señora) doesn't mention anything to me about bathing since I do shower three times a week.

> The fact is that my señora has never told me that she expects me to bathe at all . . . so I don't know how often she expects me to take a bath.

> Here there is no one telling you to keep your room neat like at "X" college or to tell you to take a bath or anything. The attitude is "live and let live" instead of this up-tight situation we had back on campus.

It is interesting to note that this type of guest feels emancipated either because he feels that the norms don't exist or that as a foreign guest he is not required to conform to the norm. He simply takes advantage of the etiquette barrier between host and guest to do as he pleases.

The third type of guest is the one who would like to bathe much more frequently but cannot surmount the barriers to communication involved in taking the necessary practical steps to get a hot bath. Taking a cold shower is unpleasant where a home can be chilly even for a person who is dry and fully dressed. Often the bathroom is not heated. Interviews with the North American guests revealed several real and assumed obstacles to taking a bath. Some of the guests thought that the family expected them to take their baths in cold water.

> Bogotá doesn't have much water, particularly hot water. Taking a cold bath at six in the morning doesn't appeal to me too much.

> The only thing that I really miss in the way of luxuries is having hot water. I've gotten so that cold showers don't bother me at all. I can wash my hair in cold water at night and it doesn't bother me at all.

> I've gotten so I take showers when I feel like it; no matter whether the water is hot or cold.

> They have hot water in the home, but they don't let me use it for showers.

There are problems I was expecting because things are not quite so modern here as at home. For instance, we haven't had hot water for about a month. At first it was terrible having to take showers at six in the morning, but I'm getting used to it. But what does sort of bug me is that they don't do anything about it. They complain, "Oh, it's terrible!" but they don't bother to call anyone or get on it and get something accomplished. I guess that hot water is just not that important to them.

When there is hot water in the morning, I generally take a shower. But there was one week when there was not any hot water at any time and I had a cold, so I went down and asked the maid (the señora had left the house) to light the thing for me. First, I tried to light it myself and when I couldn't I asked her. She said, "No, I can't do it without the señora's permission." Then she said, *"Es elegante"* meaning "You are elegant" to want a bath in hot water. I said that I can't be elegant if I only want a bath one time during the week.

Some of the guests assumed that there was never any hot water in the home and that the family either did not have a water heater or did not use it. Others realized that there was hot water at times but thought that the family either did not care enough to order the new tanks of gas or that there were severe restrictions on the use of hot water for bathing. According to the señoras, there was hot water but the guest tried to take a shower in the afternoon when the water heater was turned off or in the morning immediately after the supply had been exhausted by those who took baths earlier.

Also, Colombian hosts and their North American guests define *hot* differently. When the host said there was hot water, the guest said it was cold or only tepid at best. In one situation, the guest said, "The señora always turns off the water heater before the water can get really hot." The opposite view was expressed by the host: "The student always turns on the hot water heater a couple of hours before he takes a bath. The water would be boiling by that time."

Vignettes of Cross-Cultural Miscommunication

Actually, the host families cited above did not expect the guests to bathe in cold water, but some of the families expected the guest to use only slightly warm water. The following *vignettes* illustrate miscommunication or noncommunication. Each has as its title the false conclusion drawn by the North American. The interview excerpts and discussion are to illuminate the underlying assumptions and the information, received through direct observation or conversation, which led him to the false conclusion.

"They don't bathe in hot water in this home"

The first night I was here I took a shower at 8:30 right after dinner. Wow! What a deal! First, there was practically no water because the maid was washing dishes downstairs, and when you did really get a shot of water, it was so cold it made you jump. I thought I had gotten an unlucky break and had been placed in one of those homes where they never have any hot water. After all, if they didn't even have the hot water heater lit for washing the dishes in the evening, then they certainly wouldn't use hot water for bathing. One night the señora said to me, "Do you prefer cold showers at night?" I didn't want to complain so I said, "I don't mind cold showers at all"; so she said, "All the family takes showers in the morning." All I thought was, "That's great, just great, what could be better than crawling out of a warm bed into an icy cold shower!" I didn't accept this as a suggestion but just as an interesting piece of information until one day I talked to somebody at CEUCA who said he always had *warm* showers at his Colombian home but only in the mornings. I began to wonder if my señora had been hinting that I should take a warm shower rather than just saying the family bathed in the morning. Well, I checked up and sure enough it was a fact that there was hot water in the mornings. I had just assumed that they never bathed in hot water since they didn't use hot water to wash the dinner dishes.

This vignette illustrates how a silent assumption influences the interpretation of both observations and verbal messages. The American assumed that washing dishes in hot water is as important as having hot water for a shower. The observation of the fact that the maid always washes dishes in cold water allowed the American to conclude that the señora would not want hot water to be used for bathing. Other possible logical conclusions might be that there was no hot water heater or that it was not functioning.

The conclusion that no one in the family took warm showers then became a silent assumption in the interpretation of the señora's question, "Do you prefer cold showers at night?" The American interpreted the question as if the significance were in the word *night* rather than in the word *cold* which in the señora's mind was associated with night just as *hot* water was associated with *morning*—the time when the family took their showers.

"They don't want me to use the hot water in the morning!"

The day after I arrived, I got up early and took a hot shower. It felt great! Just like at home! I had heard from some of the other trainees that there often is not much water pressure and maybe no hot water, so you have to bathe in a dribble of cool water. This was not the case in my Colombian home. But later that day after breakfast when I was leaving to come to CEUCA, the señora asked me if it was a custom for *norteamericanos* to spend a long time in the shower. Over the next few days I noticed that the rest of the family all took baths in the morning. Well, that seemed sensible enough for me to take my bath in the evening, because the señora had been giving me a gentle hint not to bathe in the morning.

Actually, the señora was not trying to get the guest to take a bath in the evening but was hinting for him not to spend so much *time* in the bath. The North American assumed that taking a hot shower is not merely a way to get clean but is a form of rest and relaxation. The guest thought that the señora was trying to tell him that he had interfered with others taking a bath in the morning in spite of the fact that he had gotten up early specifically to take his bath at 6:30. In most of the host families this time would directly conflict with the señor's bathtime. The señora did not expect the guest to bathe in the evening but to be quick or do it after the señor has left for work if he takes a little more time. To the North American it seemed preferable to take a leisurely bath in the evening rather than a hurried bath in the morning. Of course this choice is based on the assumption that there are no additional problems in getting an evening bath.

"A night bath must be in cold water!"

I don't wash my hair in the morning because I can't go out with wet hair and many times I want to shower and wash my hair at the same time, so I have gotten into the habit of taking cold showers at night. It is not so terrible once you get used to it. I know there is hot water in the morning, but it is such a rush that I just don't get involved. At first I thought I could take a warm shower in the evening, but then I discovered that the heater is lit by the maid at about 5:30 or 6:00 in the morning and turned off at about 9:00. At first I thought it might be like the old style "rápido" heaters in Guanajuato which used coal or wood for fuel and did not have any thermostat, but then I saw that this was an automatic gas heater but they still turned it off. It was obvious that they didn't want to keep the water hot all day, and it would be very inefficient to have to heat the whole tank for just my bath. But I still had the choice of a warm bath in the morning or a cold one at night.

For many North Americans evening bathing is preferable, but this idea would have to be suggested by the guest since to many of the *bogotano* families evening would not seem to be the natural time for a bath. In this vignette no conversation contributed to the false conclusion that this particular señora did not want the guest to take a bath at night. The conclusion is an interpretation of detailed observations based on the assumption that turning off an automatic water heater at nine in the morning indicates an urgent need to save gas. Since the guest "knew" that the señora wouldn't approve of turning on the gas in the evening, she avoided embarrassment by not asking. Even though she had become accustomed to cold baths, she took fewer than she would if the water were hot.

"A night bath must be in cold water."

This guest arrives at the same conclusion as the guest in the preceding vignette but through a different major and minor premise.

> I had already heard that in some of the homes they didn't mind if you turned on the water heater to take a bath at night. That is when I usually take a bath. I just hate to get in bed when I feel dirty and sticky. It helps me get to sleep if I take a shower just before hitting the sack. So I thought I had nothing to lose if I asked the señora. She said that it would be perfectly all right for me to turn on the heater and take my bath at 9:00. She also said that since the maid might already be in her room by that time, I should turn it on myself. She even took me and showed me how to turn it on.

> Well, everything went well the first two nights when I had a great hot shower with plenty of water pressure because no one was using any water downstairs. But the morning after that second glorious bath she saw me just as I was leaving for CEUCA and dropped the remark that when she saw the water heater was on she realized that I had taken a hot bath both nights and that uses a lot of gas. It was also clear from our conversation that I should not do it again.

The señora told the Colombian interviewer that she had told the guest it was all right to take a bath at night and showed him how to turn the heater on when he needed it, but she added:

> I shouldn't have done that because he took advantage of it and would never turn the heater off after his bath. He just didn't want to come downstairs again after his bath. I told him the maid would be in bed at that time of night, so he knew she couldn't turn it off for him.

The guest apparently felt that the señora had reversed her decision. When the interviewer asked, "Why did she do that?" he explained:

> I have heard that Latin Americans in just being polite to a guest will offer things they don't really expect the person to accept. I realized that at the time but when she took me and showed me how to light the heater, I assumed that she was really expecting me to do it, but after her remarks I just didn't know what to think. I guess that instead of cutting out all of the evening baths I could have asked her if it would be all right if I took a bath just every other night. But I didn't want to push the point.

The nub of this misunderstanding is that the señora was intending to convey her disapproval of leaving the heater on all night, but the guest felt that she was expressing displeasure over his having had hot showers two nights in succession. The underlying assumption in the American's mind seemed to be that if it is permissible to turn the heater on at 9:00 p.m. and hot water is needed the next morning for showers, there is no need to turn it off at 10:00 p.m. The Colombian would point out that it would not ordinarily be turned on until 6:00 a.m., so it is a waste to leave it on the eight hours when no one could possibly be using it.

The analysis of these cases of miscommunication shows that when the person is required to *act* but does not understand the culturally patterned possibilities of action in that situation, he applies his own culturally determined assumptions to fill the vacuum. Although he can see and hear that certain things are different from the pattern to which he is accustomed, this information in the raw form is often not enough to guide his action; so he must interpret the information and transform it into actionable terms. Assumptions that describe the range of the permissible patterns and the priorities of the preferred patterns of action would be most useful. Insofar as the actor is ignorant of these realities in the foreign culture, he unconsciously fills this knowledge vacuum with the assumptions brought with him from the United States.

The Host-Family Bathing Pattern

— This description is based upon a logically systematic sifting of the bathing problems as described by the American guests and the Colombian hosts. In the dimensions of the Colombian pattern where there are alternative paths of action we emphasize the one that does not coincide with the North American pattern.

Daily bath. The Colombians bathe daily and expect their guests to do the same.

Shower. Typically, there is no bath tub but a shower.

Water temperature. What seems like an adequate supply of warm water to the Colombian often does not seem so to the North American guests who prefer hotter water and more of it for bathing.

Morning bathing. Most Colombian families bathe in the morning, and hot water is almost always available at this time. Even though hot water is not normally available in the evenings, some families prefer to make it available for the guest in the evening to avoid congestion in the bathroom in the morning.

Evening bathing. If it is permissible to take a bath in the evening, the guest should have a clear arrangement regarding who is to turn the heater *on* and *off* and at what time.

Soap and towel. Guests are expected to furnish their own bath towel and soap.

Place for toilet articles. Guests are expected to keep soap and towel as well as all other toilet articles in their bedroom closets. Exceptions to this are where either the guest or the parents have their own private bathroom.

Hanging towel in sun. Guests are usually expected to hang their towels out to dry in the patio in the morning. Guests may be expected to ask the maid to do it.

Conserving water and towels. Bathing should be accomplished with as little strain on the supply of hot water and towels as possible. It is difficult to dry towels in the Bogotá climate, and hot water is not only relatively expensive but the bottled gas upon which it depends is subject to periodic shortages. Also if the gas is exhausted ahead of schedule, it may take two to four weeks to get delivery.

Mode of dress. The preferred mode of dress for going to and from the bath is pajamas, slippers, and bathrobe.

Soiled clothes. The host families usually expect the guest to leave his soiled clothes which are to be washed by the family maid neatly folded on the floor, bed or chair in his bedroom. Most families clearly expect the female guest to wash her own undergarments, and these things are to be kept out of sight in the guest's bedroom closet.

Dry bathroom. Guests are expected to leave the floor dry in the bathroom after a shower. This is best done by prevention rather than mopping up afterward.

Tidy bathroom. To the señora "tidy" means that any person using the bathroom should not leave any signs of their having been there or objects such as razor blades, hair curlers, towels, lipstick, powder, soap, hair oil. The female guests must keep in mind that in most households the plumbing system is not designed to accommodate Kotex or Tampax, which will often plug the system, causing considerable inconvenience and expense. It should be carefully wrapped and put in the appropriate wastebasket.

The more guests know of the pattern before getting into the Colombian home the better, because discovering the pattern may take days and sometimes weeks. This allows time for considerable mis-understanding to arise, for false conclusions to be drawn by both the hosts and the guests, for the relationship to be profoundly influenced, and for attitudes to be set.

In some extreme cases in our study, the señora reported that she would never have another North American guest in her home because of small inconveniences and conflicts that constantly arose with the guest. Typically, the North American guest was not aware of much of the conflict and strain he was causing in the family. In one case the family found the situation becoming so intolerable that they called the student advisor at CEUCA, a Colombian woman, to ask that the girl be removed from their home. When the student advisor called the girl in for a conference, the girl insisted that she should not be moved to another family because she was "loved like a member of the family." While the two were still in conference at CEUCA, the father of the host family called to be reassured that the girl would be "taken to another family immediately." That same afternoon the girl went home and asked the señora (contrary to the advice of the student advisor) why they did not want her in their home any longer. When the señora said they had been perfectly happy with her, the girl wrote a letter to this effect and had the señora sign it and then presented this letter to the Dean of Women on her home campus in the United States as evidence that she was being unjustly removed from the family she loved. This reluctance to say to someone, particularly a guest, "You are dirty," or "You are immoral," or "You are arrogant," is not a unique characteristic of the "Latin character" but can be seen often in the United States.

Notes

1. We do not intend to convey the idea that a *majority* of the host homes had no stoppers in the sinks and lavatories; we only know that this was a complaint of *some* American guests, but the question was not systematically asked of all of them.

4

The Bedroom

Some of the differences surrounding the bedroom may seem insignificant because no single one is the cause of great cross-cultural confusion. However, collectively they form the backdrop for the guest–host interaction and lend an atmosphere of ambiguity to the scene. At first the North American may be annoyed or confused by some of these differences, then he adjusts his behavior to them so that the initial negative response may be reduced. This reduction of anxiety often lulls the guest into a false sense of satisfaction with his "savoir faire." He may feel that he has arrived at an understanding of the Colombian home at a time when he has just begun to cause the Colombian host considerable annoyance, anxiety, or even hostility in extreme cases.

Physical Characteristics

Typically, the host homes have all of the bedrooms upstairs except for the maid's. The downstairs is assumed to be less secure from robbery and less comfortable because the sun's warmth does not penetrate during the day. Even though the upstairs is generally warmer, 62 percent of the North American guests felt that their bedrooms were uncomfortably cold at times, and only 2 percent had any form of heat in their rooms. The Colombians wear warmer woolen clothing inside the house and a wool bathrobe, warm pajamas, and slippers in their bedrooms. Still they find it necessary upon occasion to get under the covers to be comfortable while they read after dinner. Some North Americans report that they have adjusted by wearing more clothes than they would in the United States where there is central heating. They might wear a *ruana* while sitting in their room; some wear socks to sleep in; others seem to have very little problem because their homes are situated on *carreras* which have considerable exposure to the sun during the day. In any case, the adjustment to indoor temperature seems to be a universal initial problem of the North American in Bogotá.

Another source of initial annoyance for the American is the lighting, particularly in his bedroom. First, he might have difficulty finding the light switch. It is usually outside the door to the room, but this is only a reminder of the more frustrating fact that the lighting seems entirely inadequate to the American who is accustomed to a much greater intensity. He is initially surprised then adjusts, but he relapses into frustration when he tries to pick out the proper pair of socks in a drawer or discovers that he has put on a pair of trousers that do not match his coat. A more serious effect of the reduced lighting is found when he tries to study in his room. Only 34 percent of the Americans had a special reading light of any kind in their room, and 69 percent felt that the lighting was inadequate for studying. Only 38 percent of the American students had a desk or table of any kind in their room, and 60 percent of them felt that these facilities were less convenient than they were accustomed to in the United States. Where the American was occupying the same room the Colombian son or daughter had occupied the previous year, the American sometimes falsely assumed that the family had taken out the desk and reading light. This was usually not the case since Colombian students do very little studying in their bedrooms at home in the evening.

Usually there is a crucifix on the wall at the head of the bed. Most American guests did not have any objection to the presence of the crucifix; others had a private feeling of mild objection or amusement; and a very small minority (about 2 percent mentioned this in an interview) actively objected to it and to religious pictures the señora placed in the room, apparently for the guest's benefit.

A more minor detail that seemed to annoy the American guest was the lack of a wastebasket in his room. This becomes more puzzling to the American guest when he discovers that his host expects him to keep his room "spic and span" at all times. In the United States, wastebaskets are much more in evidence in various corners of a home and are much more essential because of the greater consumption of paper—packaging, junk mail, and reading material—and the absence of a maid who regularly picks up the waste paper that is left around.

Another minor detail is the lack of a radio in the guest's room. Only a few of the host homes furnished a radio in the guest's room. Most of the Americans did not bring one because they wanted to travel lightly, and they discovered that radios were too expensive to buy in Colombia. This is unfortunate because the radio is one of the very important windows to the Colombian culture. It is clearly the major medium of mass communication and has not been relegated to a lower position of importance by television and printed materials as in the United States.

A few of the Americans missed having their own record players in their rooms. In the American culture the record player is thought of as a form of individual entertainment. The young child, the teenager, and the parents have completely different collections of records and tend to listen to them at different times and places. In contrast, the host families thought of the record player as a necessary item in any *fiesta bailable* in the home. Therefore, it was almost always located in the living room.

The temperature of the room; the location of light switches; the reduced lighting; the presence of the crucifix; and the relative absence of desk, chairs, wastebaskets, radios, and record players are all superficial reminders of the fact that one is a guest in a foreign country. The American guest usually adjusts to these overt physical inconveniences quickly, but it takes him much longer to discover those *covert* assumptions regarding the *use* of the bedroom.

Confusion and Conflict over Bedmaking

The American guest with the best of intentions and goodwill often gives the Colombian host the impression that he is lazy, sloppy, and demanding—if not downright arrogant—because he is confused by what we have come to call the "silent battle of the bed." Some of the American guests began making their own beds the first morning either because they thought it was the proper thing to do as a "good long-term guest," or they did not like the way it was made the first night and wanted to make it their own way. One frequent objection is that the bed is made without tucking in either the top sheet or the covers at the bottom, and the American finds that the covers keep coming off in the middle of the night and he is cold. He makes his own bed but notices that it is remade each day. He interprets this as a gentle hint that he should *not* do it himself but leave it for the maid to do.

> I don't know how the Colombians ever sleep at night and keep the covers on if the beds are always made like they are in my house. But when I did it myself the first week, the maid did it over again her way. So, naturally, I took the hint and quit making the bed. Later, I learned from some of the other CEUCA students and Peace Corps Trainees that they had been warned that they shouldn't try to do the maid's work. What I finally did was just let the maid do it, but at night when I got in bed I would tuck the sheet and blankets under the mattress at the foot of the bed so that the covers would not be off in the morning. Then in the morning I would take them out again so that they wouldn't know that I was such a peculiar person.

Other American guests did not make their beds from the start because they felt that it was the maid's job which they should not usurp. Actually a clear majority of the Colombian host families felt that the guest, particularly the female guest, should make her own bed. The fact that most of the señoras did not think the guest made a bed properly accounts for why when the guest tried to make his own bed, he found it had been done over again. Communication often broke down because the American thought the host was hinting that he should not make the bed himself, but the host was actually trying to show him how to make the bed properly.

> As you know, in the States the girls make their own beds, but the ones I have had never worried about it. The first day they tried to make it by just putting their bedspread over the top, so then I really made it well, but then they never worried about it again.

> I change the sheets every week and the guests don't have to do anything except make their own beds. But I learned not to let them do it themselves because they don't do it properly.

> He wouldn't make the bed because he knew that you would make it for him.

> One time, for example, there wasn't a maid and Diana didn't make the bed and at lunch time it still wasn't made, so in the evening I called her and told her that she should realize that there was not a maid (for the upstairs) and to help me to straighten her room and to make the bed.

> One of the couples didn't make their bed well. I made it for them because I don't like to see a bed that is not well made.

> She wouldn't make her bed and I didn't think it was correct because at that time I had only one maid, but I never told her about it because I think it was the maid's fault because she would tell Jane not to make the bed, but the maid would not make it either. I'd come to the house and find it unmade, so I told Michelle to tell the girl that my own daughters make their beds and I thought she should do the same thing.

Careful comparison of many remarks by students and señoras show that, despite some variation from one family to another in their expectations regarding bedmaking, there is a general pattern in the conflict of silent assumptions.

American Assumptions	Colombian Assumptions
Most Colombian families expect the maid to make all the beds in the home.	Most teenagers and adults are expected to make their own beds. This is particularly true of the females. Only in a very few households where there are at least two and perhaps three maids would a guest not be "allowed" to make his own bed.
It is a nice gesture for the female guest to make her own bed, but it is not really expected.	Regardless of the number of maids, most families expect the females to make their own beds.
When I don't make the bed myself, it is always the maid who makes it.	If the bed is not made by the guest, the señora will often make it herself to avoid complaints from the maid who does not consider this her job.
It is not important how I make the bed as long as I can sleep in it. It is a waste of valuable time to be so meticulous about the appearance of the bedroom which, after all, is private.	It is important to make the bed well so that it will not damage the overall appearance of neatness in the bedroom when visitors in the home see it. An untidy appearance of the bedroom reflects upon my (the señora's) reputation.

The dissonance between the American's and the Colombian's assumptions, then, involves two basic dimensions of the social situation. One is the role of the maid and the other is the conception of the bedroom as a public versus a private area.

The "Open Door" Policy

Some misunderstandings between the American guest and Colombian host hinge upon the basic differences in their assumptions regarding the function of a bedroom. Both cultures accept the bedroom as a place to sleep, to make conjugal love, and to read, but beyond that there is little agreement. The American thinks of it (particularly when he is in a foreign country) as a place to retreat, to find privacy, to study, to listen to records. The Colombian host families did not agree on all these things. The señora thinks of her bedroom as being a place to socialize with her friends, to watch television with members of the family and with friends. In Bogotá the television viewing is in the evening because the programs do not begin until 5:30 or 6:00 p.m.

Although the Colombian university student is much more likely than his American counterpart to live at home (since universities rarely have dormitories), he is not expected to spend much time studying in his bedroom. The Colombian student does less studying anywhere because he spends much more time in class and in traveling to and from the university than his United States counterpart. The class load for Colombian students in Bogotá ranges from 25 to 42 hours per week, and many students spend from 10 to 20 hours per week traveling between their home (or a relative's home or student *pension*) and the university. This totals from 35 to 62 hours per week before allowing time for essentials such as meals and socializing, which leaves little time for studying.

The Colombian student may frequently study with friends in a public place such as a restaurant, coffee house, or library. Only rarely does he spend long hours studying in his room.

In contrast to this, the North American student has more time to study because his class load, even in Colombia, is likely to range between 14 and 17 hours per week. Since he is a foreign student, has some difficulty with the language, and does not have the background knowledge to compete easily with the Colombian student, he must do more studying outside of class than his Colombian fellow student. The North American has both the opportunity and the need to study more. Furthermore, the North American students show a strong preference for their own room as a place to study.

The daily activity pattern of the North American is quite different from that of a Colombian university student. This difference is usually not understood by the Colombian host family who might think of the American guest as being an overstudious person or a recluse who hides out in his room to avoid Colombians.

Some of the señoras appreciated the North American's need to study more than Colombian students and others did not. Seventy percent of the host-family señoras thought the American student studied *too much*. A few of the señoras said that they thought that studying was just an excuse to avoid associating with the Colombian family. Almost half of the señoras felt that the guests wanted to be alone more than they should.

This general image of the American guest as being aloof is not the result of any single act such as studying in his room. This image is reinforced by other actions (or lack of action) the Colombian interprets as manifestations of the same basic tendency for self-segregation by the American. For example, 55 percent felt that the American guests do not greet people properly.[1] Consistent with these images, 45 percent of the families also felt that the Americans are "generally thoughtless of others." Sixty-three percent of the host families felt that the Americans "think they are superior to Colombians," and 72 percent of the Colombian hosts thought that the Americans "feel that the United States is superior to Colombia."

Of course these negative images are the result of the Colombians' observations, interpretations, or misinterpretations of their guests' behavior.

The señora thinks of her bedroom as a place to socialize in the afternoons with friends, relatives, and neighbors. Her bedroom door was usually open during the day when she was home, and it was also usually left open when she went out of the house. American guests who spent time in their rooms with the door closed were thought of as introverted.

> I really wonder why she came to Colombia. She was introverted (*reconcentrada*). She was not at all sociable.

> I would say that she was a kind girl but a difficult person. She was a little introverted. I don't think she adjusted to her environment.

> He was very nice and pleasant. The only thing was that when he came in the house, he shut himself in his room, but that was just a question of personality.

> Donna did not like children. She would confine herself to her room and not let the children in. She spoke little and was not sociable at all.

> When we would have a party at our house, she would say hello to the people who came, stay a little while, and then leave for her bedroom.

Some of the señoras realized that this tendency to retreat was not a sign of the American's feeling of superiority or dislike for Colombians, but that it resulted from a certain amount of nervous strain in interacting with foreigners even when there is no language barrier.

> He spoke very good Spanish, but he was timid and a little introverted. At the beginning he would have his dinner and then watch television and go to his room to study. He finally adapted to our customs, but it was hard for him.

> Mary was very nervous. Sometimes when she was invited, she would even perspire because she was so nervous about going and meeting people. She was very timid. When she was invited to go to a party with us, she would say, "Are you sure I won't be a bother to you? Do they really want me to come?" And I'd tell her that they had really invited her to come. I explained that if my own daughters had not been invited I wouldn't be taking them.

Although most of the señoras thought the Americans studied too much, a sizable minority clearly admired the studiousness of their guests.

> I find this a good quality in the American students. They want to study, to investigate, and to know more. That doesn't happen with us Colombians; we are

lazy. In general the North American student studies. He dedicates himself to studying and assumes the responsibility to obtain more knowledge.

I think they are more studious and more responsible than Colombians.

They really want to learn. We would like our own children to be this way!

Apparently those Colombians who empathize with the difficulty of interacting spontaneously with foreigners, who also recognize that the American must study harder to make up for the lack of background knowledge, and who know that the student is actually studying behind that closed door are more willing to forgive the American for "hiding in his room."

Even though the señora can understand why the student may have to study, she does not think the door should be closed unless it is necessary to exclude noise and interruptions from outside. She does not believe it should be closed merely to prevent being seen in one's room by family members or visitors. When a person encounters a closed door in a situation where his cultural background calls for the open door policy, there is usually a negative reaction. This is illustrated by Hall's account of a business situation where the American in contrast to the German is more accustomed to the open door policy.

> The open door policy of American business and the closed door patterns of German business culture cause clashes in the branches and subsidiaries of American firms in Germany. I was once called to advise a firm that has operations all over the world. One of the first questions asked was, "How do you get the Germans to keep their doors open?" In this company the open doors were making the German feel exposed and gave the whole operation an unusually relaxed and unbusinesslike air. Closed doors, on the other hand, gave the Americans the feeling that there was a conspiratorial air about the place and that they were being left out.[2]

In this German–American business setting, it is the American who is on the side of the open door policy, while in the Colombian–American home setting, the Colombian is more clearly on the side of the open door policy.

The importance of leaving the bedroom door open was demonstrated when the señoras were asked, "If a friend of your North American guest came to visit him in the afternoon, where would you prefer that they visit?" Sixty-three percent said they should entertain in the living room; 24 percent said in the guest's bedroom with the door *open*; and a few said in the guest's bedroom with the door *closed*, in the second floor hall, or in some other place. When the question was asked in Spanish, it was clear that we were referring to a visiting friend of the same sex. When the question was asked about a visiting friend of the opposite sex, *none* preferred them to visit in the guest's bedroom with or without the door closed.

The door shouldn't be closed for long.

[The door should not be closed] if there is no noise around.

I would allow it but I think they shouldn't.

There is no need to close the door.

[They can entertain] in any place except in the bedroom with the door closed, because there is no reason for them to lock themselves up.

If he is a close friend, it would be better to visit in the señora's bedroom.

It might be permissible if I knew what kind of friendship there was between them.

They could close the door only if they were studying.

The open door policy is preferred even though the precise reason for this is not clear.

Even though some of the American guests discovered this preference for the open door, they were more inclined to leave the door open while they were out of the room than when they were in it.

Some of the American guests complained that while they were away during the day, the small children in the home went through all their belongings in the room, obviously out of curiosity since only rarely was some small thing missing. The señora probably locks the closet doors or some of the drawers in her room when she leaves the house, but she does usually leave the door of her bedroom open.

The Open Door and Guest-Host Conflict

If the American guest keeps his door closed in the afternoons or evenings when he is not sleeping, he will probably be considered anti-social. Yet for some guests to practice the "open door policy" would be opening Pandora's Box by allowing visual contact between the *bogotano* middle-class adult culture and the American middle-class student culture. If the room is a mess according to *bogotano* standards, the situation not only shocks the señora's aesthetic sensibilities but may also threaten her social standing in the community.

The whole upstairs, including the guest's bedroom, is as open to friends, relatives, and neighbors as is the downstairs living room. Since she often holds court in her own bedroom in the afternoons and early evenings, her visitors may pass the guest's bedroom door. The hostess's reputation as a good housekeeper, as a person who can control the maid and obtain the respect of the guest, may suffer if the appearance of the guest's room is not tidy.

Slightly more than half of the señoras evaluated the neatness of their guests favorably. The areas of concern to them were bodily cleanliness, tidiness in the use of the bathroom, orderliness in the bedroom, and dress. Males were generally thought of as being neater and cleaner than females, particularly in the use of the bedroom.

Fifty-two percent of the señoras agreed that the American guest "doesn't care about his reputation among the Colombians."[3] Yet the responses to the statement, "They don't care if they damage the reputation of the Colombian families" (25 percent agreed) shows that the Colombians did recognize that the American guest was concerned about the reputation of his Colombian family even though he did not always behave in a way to protect his own reputation among the Colombians. However, even though Colombians recognize that guests do have some concern for the family's reputation, they are not always successful in protecting it. Often this is because the American does not know how to do it, nor does the Colombian know how to persuade the American that certain of his actions reflect upon the Colombian family's reputation. Sometimes the guest tries to protect the family's reputation by keeping the door to his room closed, only to be judged as an introvert.

Almost half of the señoras agreed with the statement, "The Americans expect special care and attention from Colombians," although this is not connected exclusively with the American's behavior in the bedroom. For example, the American's use of the bedroom buzzer to summon the maid is considered inappropriate under many circumstances. Since we did not concentrate on this problem, we do not know *who* is expected to use the buzzer *when* for what *purpose*, but a guest who is sick might make arrangements with the señora to buzz for the maid during the day if something is needed.

The misunderstanding regarding who is supposed to make the bed is also a source of the señora's feeling that the American expects extra attention and special services not performed for regular members of the family. The señoras interpreted the American's sloppiness in the bedroom as an indication that he expects special picking up services which would not be rendered to other members of the family.

> With Lisa I had a lot of problems and I think she did it *just to be bad* because she understood that she was not doing the correct thing. Once she said, "I'm going to give you a present." What was the present? She tidied up her room. She was generally very untidy.

> The problem with the girls I had was that they were unclean and untidy. The last one I had was worse than all the rest, so I have *decided not to have one in my home again.*

> She was untidy in her room and was *very demanding* about her room being tidy, but she wouldn't do anything herself. She would take her clothes off and throw

them down anywhere. She would fill the ashtray and have it full of ashes for three or four days, but she wouldn't empty it. She would be disgusted because the maid wouldn't tidy her room, but she would not take care of her things. But in her own *personal* appearance she was very, very tidy and well dressed.

Dorothy was not so tidy so you had to pick things up. . . . She just left her things around her room. She would get dressed very quickly and leave things lying around. I would advise her not to do that because *somebody* would come to her room or to the library (upstairs) and they would find things untidy.

When John came, he was very untidy. He would leave his shoes around and then I'd tidy his room and then ten minutes later the room was all upset again, so I'd tell him to put everything in its place and he didn't get angry with me and he learned. I still made the bed for him.

The one that I have now is very untidy in the sense that whatever she takes off she leaves on the floor instead of taking her clothes and hanging them up so that when she wants to wear them again they will be ready. Every time she has to wear something, it is so creased that she has to come down and iron it. In the morning you have to straighten her room for her, but she has the obligation as well as my daughters to keep the room tidy and she doesn't. I told her but she doesn't obey me. I think that is born into the people.

I do not think any American is clean and tidy. She was so untidy and fortunately I am an extremely tidy person. The room they were using, which was my daughter's bedroom, was just like a mad house. Nothing was in its place. The powder was here, a shoe there, and a book in another place. It was absolutely terrible. They are not tidy at all and in spite of the fact that she saw the tidiness in the rest of the house, I let them keep the room the way they are accustomed to, but they *did not make any effort* to keep it nice. I'd tell my daughter to tell them that our customs were not the same and that they had to keep things in place.

These statements are of course only the negative ones which might throw some light on the negative images. It is interesting to note that many of the statements show that it was the señora who did the picking up rather than the maid. Some señoras mentioned that they tried to correct the guest's behavior, but generally the señora did not feel that the advice was heeded seriously. In some cases the señora tried *indirectly* to correct the guest's behavior.

Although the señora feels that the guest should not be a hermit in his room with the door closed, she is subjected to considerable anxiety when the guest follows the open-door policy. She tends to follow a pattern of first setting an example by keeping the rest of the house orderly. If this has no effect on the guest's behavior, she straightens the room herself, again hoping that the guest will take the hint. This is usually ineffective either because the guest does not care about the impression he makes, because he does not realize that his untidy room is viewed by the señora as a challenge to her social status, or because he thinks the maid straightens up his room as part of her usual duties for any member of the family. This conflicting assumption causes the señora to perceive the guest as "demanding." The American guest's view was succinctly stated by one guest when he said, "They don't clean my room, and there is a maid. I even have to clean my bathroom. It is not that serious, *but what's that maid for?"*

Even when the señora *directly* suggests to the guest that the messy room is upsetting to her and that the guest should do something about it personally, she often feels that her suggestions fall on deaf ears as far as she can determine from the results. We do not know whether the señora was able to be clear enough to impress the American with the fact that he was being *advised.* Some of the Americans felt the bedroom was their own private area, and how they kept it was either their own business or that it was the maid's fault for not keeping it in better order for them.

We do not know what proportion of the host families decided not to take another American guest because of the unpleasantness of the culture shock at various focal points of the collision between the middle-class, adult *bogotano* culture and the middle-class United States student culture. We can be sure that this culture shock caused some of the host families' decisions to withdraw.

The Closed Closet Solution

Once the sensitive and mature American guest became aware of the señora's distress over the appearance of his room and he became convinced that the solution was not simply to keep his door shut, he would compromise by throwing everything in the closet to keep it out of sight. There was considerable impressionistic evidence that this was appreciated by the señora as an attempt to protect her reputation. What the American guest did not realize was that it often did not improve her image of his character when the result was merely a more disarranged closet. The Americans seemed to assume that "out of sight was out of mind," but many of the señoras were aware enough of the internal condition of the guest's closet to pass judgment upon it.

> She was very tidy and very clean in her closet. She'd wear a dress for two or three times and then she'd send it out to the cleaners.
>
> They didn't keep their closet very tidy.
>
> Patty was untidy at the beginning and later she wasn't. Sometimes she'd leave things around and I'd tell her that she had a big closet and to keep everything in her closet so that you couldn't see anything around the bedroom.
>
> He was very tidy about his closet. When for example, Amparo would come into

the room to take the dirty clothes, he would say, "Please tell me where are you going to put them," and he'd take them down.

She would put her dirty underwear in the closet and then from time to time she would wash it.

The only thing he was a little untidy about was his closet. His clothes were not very well arranged in the drawers, and also he'd leave books untidy.

I do not think any American is clean or tidy. The closet was all untidy and mixed. They are not tidy at all and in spite of the fact that she saw the tidiness in the rest of the house.

The guests knew that the señoras were aware of the state of the closets and, in some cases, were trying to drop a hint to the American who often responded by feeling that his privacy was being invaded.

They go through everything we own every day, and when we put things away in a different drawer than they like, they change it. Nothing is ever harmed, but obviously it is moved around and examined.

.If I leave anything in the bathroom, except the washcloth, it ends up in my closet.

I know that people have looked through things in my drawers. It is just that there is a lack of privacy.

The *Bogotano* Pattern of Neatness in the Closet

The perceptive American guest sees that he must come to terms with the fact that the señora is not pleased with keeping the bedroom door shut, nor is she pleased to have the door open for visitors to see the room in disarray. Furthermore, tossing everything into the closet in a disorganized fashion may reduce the threat to the señora's reputation, which she seems to appreciate, but it does not save the image of the American guest's character in her eyes. Sometimes only reluctantly does the American guest arrive at the realization that the cultural pattern calls for neatness all the way. What, then, is the pattern expected by the *bogotano* family? Every host family did not rigidly adhere to every item in this pattern, but most families did adhere strongly to most of the items. The guest's observance of *all* of them would not have caused friction and would definitely have improved his image and relationship to the family.

In addition to the expectations with regard to bedmaking, the following expectations apply to the neatness of the room.

The open door. The guest should leave his bedroom door open during the day unless he is dressing or unless noise from the hall would seriously disturb him while studying. When the guest is out of the house, the bedroom door should also be open. If the guest would like to protect certain valuable items such as a camera from damage by curious children or maids, he could keep it in a locked drawer or closet.

The orderly bedroom. The room should appear neat at all times. All clothes should be hung in the closet, never on the bed, under the bed, hanging over chairs, or on the floor. Shoes and slippers should not be kept on the floor, under the bed, on top of the night stand, or in any location where they are visible or interfere with sweeping the room. Reading materials and study materials should not be left in disarray on the bed, night table, or desk but should at least be neatly rearranged on the desk or table. It would be preferable to put them out of sight in a drawer or shelf in the closet. Underclothes that are drying after being hand-washed by the guests should be hung in the patio.

The closed closet. The closet should be kept closed when not in use, and its contents should be neatly arranged.

The buzzer. The guest is generally not expected to use the buzzer in his room except under certain "emergency conditions."

The señora's reputation. Many of the señoras feel that a disorderly bedroom reflects upon their ability as *dueña de casa* and their ability to control the maid or to gain the respect of the guest.

The señora's responsibility. When the señora notices that the guest's room is disorderly, she usually prefers to straighten it up herself rather than simply to shut the door. Usually the señora, rather than the maid, does this extra chore.

Permissible Forms of Dress in the Bedroom

The open door policy puts not only the *room* on display but also the guest who is in the room. We asked the señoras what forms of dress they considered permissible for the male guest and the female guest while studying in their rooms with the door open. By asking the same question of both the Colombian hosts and the American guests, we were able to gauge the extent to which the guests were accurately aware of the expectations of the hosts.

Females were more aware of what was expected than males, probably because the señora who rules the house is more willing to correct the female guest than the male guest. The female guest is also more frequently willing to ask the señora for advice on dress and has more opportunity to observe the behavior of the señora since she is at home more than the señor.

Guests tend to underestimate the host's preference for the more conservative dress. Or, to put it another way, they generally over-estimated the señora's permissiveness, even after living with the family from six weeks to six months. The largest overestimate of the señora's permissiveness is in the matter of going barefooted.

Although the following standards would not be expected by all host families, we can feel fairly sure that no *bogotano* would feel offended by them. Good cross-cultural strategy would suggest that the guest begin with this more conservative position and maintain it unless it is clear either by word or deed of the host that certain deviations are considered in good taste.

Although it is perfectly permissible to be dressed for the street in one's own bedroom, this is not viewed as "being at home" or "being comfortable." To be "comfortable" the woman may be in a dress, blouse and skirt, or blouse and slacks. The man may simply take off his jacket (or sweater) and tie, or he may also take off his street shoes and substitute house slippers or sandals.

Bare feet are not acceptable. One should have on house slippers or sandals. Of course street shoes would be permissible but would not be required.

If the person wants to take off all of his street clothes, the complete combination of pajamas, bathrobe, and slippers is preferred by most señoras. Never should the person be in underclothes only. Even the slip, pants, and bra combination is not acceptable.

Both dress shirts and sports shirts, with or without a tie, are acceptable for men. To be shirtless (with or without undershirt) or in under shorts only is not acceptable. The guest often discovers that if he wears no jacket or sweater in his room, he is chilly unless he puts on a bathrobe or a *ruana*.

It is important that a person not put his feet (with shoes) up on a chair, the bed or table of any kind.

There is no doubt that the Colombian pattern will appear "too restricting" to those Americans who feel the urge to liberate their toes by going barefooted or who like to get on their bed with their street shoes on or otherwise assert their freedom. This, of course, is understandable, but modes of dress of many of the American guests were considered a spectacle by the señoras and threatened their reputations. Much to the American's surprise, such decisions as whether to introduce him to certain people were made on the basis of the general appropriateness of his dress and grooming.

Most of the American students were able to adjust to these expectations and even discover that they were quite comfortable under the physical and cultural conditions in Bogotá.

Television in the Señora's Bedroom

One aspect of the señora's bedroom, that the only television set of the household was usually located there, sometimes became the focus of miscommunication. Eighty-two percent of the host homes had one television set, 3 percent had two, and the remaining 15 percent had none. Of those that had only one set, 80 percent were upstairs (70 percent in the señora's bedroom and 10 percent in the upstairs hall, library, or study), and the others were in the living room.

This pattern was the basis of miscommunication which generated negative attitudes in the guest toward the señora of the house. She was seen as selfish because the only television in the house was in her bedroom. Some guests felt that this was an important point because they wanted to watch television, and they assumed that they should not enter the señora's bedroom to see it. Others noted that the television was in the señora's bedroom but did not complain about this because they felt the television shows were not of interest to them personally.

After living with the family for two months, 25 percent of the guests had still not watched television even though at least half of these admitted to some confusion regarding when it was permissible to do so. Even after discussing it with each other, they could not find agreement; yet only two out of a group of 36 guests had attempted to question the señora to clarify the expectations of their particular host family. In only one case did the señora (who had been to the States) try to explain the situation to the guest.

Most guests realized that the señora's bedroom was much more accessible to others than would be their own mother's bedroom in the States.

> Everybody's got a T.V. set in the señora's bedroom. I've never seen a T.V. set in a Bogotá house that's in the living room.

> The whole family piles into mother's bed and watches television. For a while the T.V. was in the hall and that meant that you had to sit on the floor which was sort of uncomfortable, plus the fact that people were always clogging up the hall and it wasn't really big enough when the whole neighborhood came. Then it was in the bedroom. Everybody went in. The neighborhood boys came in to watch T.V. They all go into mom's room to watch now.

> We have a T.V. set in the parent's room. It is used very often as gathering place for the T.V. set. The parents often go into the bedroom early at night. . . . They go to bed about 8:30 or 9:00 and watch T.V., and the kids come in and watch with them and they read the paper in bed or something like that, so most of the time is spent in the bedrooms.

> She (the señora) has a friend that's a priest. The first time he came, he was

downstairs because we were just getting ready to eat. The second time we had just finished eating and he went upstairs to watch T.V. with them in the señora's bedroom.

When first encountering the fact that the only television set is in the señora's bedroom, the American sometimes thinks that this is a peculiarity of his particular host family rather than a general pattern.

They have a large living room but it's a living room and dining room combined with nothing to separate the two rooms except for the furniture arrangement. There is not a corner into which the television would fit nicely. This is the reason they have it upstairs, sometimes in the parents' bedroom, but usually it is out in the hall where they all sit in a row and watch it.

The señor is practically never home at my house. He leaves at 7:00 in the morning and doesn't get back till late and he might go right to bed. Also, since there are no children to watch T.V. it might as well be in the bedroom in this case since there is no one but the señora to watch it.

The señora in my house doesn't trust anyone to use the T.V. set so she keeps it in her own bedroom where the kids and the maid won't get to it. After all they cost a lot more here than they do in the States.

Reactions to Different Ways to Share T.V.

Even though most guests soon observed that there was no intention by the señora to monopolize the television for her exclusive use, many guests still had false assumptions regarding restrictions on its use. We asked the señoras to what extent they would consider it polite or impolite for the guest to share television in various situations, and the guests were asked to tell how they would expect their señora to respond to each of the same situations.

Situation 1: The guest goes to the señora's bedroom to watch television while she is absent. The first sharing situation was simply that of the student (sex unspecified) entering the señora's bedroom to watch television while she was out. Forty-one percent of the señoras felt that this would be a polite enough thing to do.

The student should be in a family atmosphere. It is natural for them to watch television when they wish.

I want the students to feel at home . . . so they can use the television whenever they want.

It is natural that the student goes to the señora's room to watch television, even when she is not in.

Some of the señoras qualified the instances in which it would be polite.[4]

If they watch no later than 10:30, because that is when my own children have to stop watching television.

If it is a girl that comes into the señora's bedroom while she is out, that is all right, but not if it is a boy.

First, he should ask the señora in advance if it is usually permitted.

If it is a girl and the husband is present, that would be very impolite.

In view of the lack of unanimity among the señoras regarding situation it is not surprising that 74 percent of the guests took the "neutral" position on this. For the sake of cross-cultural relations it was probably well that the guests took a cautious stance rather than optimistically assuming that since the señora's bedroom was a gathering place, anyone could enter at any time uninvited and without consideration of the sex of the guest or the possible presence of the señor.

Situation 2: At 9:30 p.m. the señora's bedroom door is open. The guest (a girl) sees that the señora is watching T.V. and without asking permission enters, sits on the bed, and watches too. The second situation had about the same degree of negative response as the first situation had positive response. The guest should have asked permission.

It might be all right if the señora has had an agreement with her from the beginning that she could come in any time the door is open.

Only if they had a relationship of mother and daughter.

It is all right for her to come in, but she should sit somewhere else, not on the bed.

It would be very uncomfortable for both of them if she did not ask permission.

At 9:30 p.m. is no proper time for the student to come into the bedroom and stay.

She must wait to be invited.

The student should at least say "hello" and then sit down to watch television.

There would be no need to ask if it were early, but not at 9:30.

A number of possible reasons make the guest's behavior inappropriate. The same behavior would have been even less acceptable in the case of a male guest.

The American guests realized that the behavior in Situation 2 would be considered impolite. Again a larger proportion of the guests than of the hosts took the "neutral" refuge because of their lack of familiarity with the expectations governing the situation.

Situation 3: The señora is watching T.V. in her bedroom at night, and the guest (a girl) knocks at the door and asks, "May I watch T.V. with you?"

Situation 4: Instead of asking directly whether she may watch television, the guest (a girl) simply looks toward the room, smiles at the señora and says, "Good evening" to see whether the señora will invite her to see the program. The significant difference between Situations 3 and 4 is that the first is a *direct* approach and the second is *indirect*. From the point of view of the Colombian host, they are equally acceptable, but from the point of view of the American guest there is a significant difference. A much smaller proportion thought that the señora would feel the indirect method to be polite. The American guests underestimated the amount of approval the señoras gave to the indirect approach. The señoras generally implied that this indirect approach would be appreciated because it gives the señora a realistic option where she is not forced to say no, but the indirect approach is usually not necessary when there is a good relationship between host and guest.

Situation 5: The guest mentions to the señora that he would like to see a certain T.V. program.

Situation 6: The guest says, "Friday night at 9:30 there is a program I would like to see, if you don't want to watch something else." The important differences between Situations 5 and 6 are in the degree of specificity as to the *time* of the program and the addition of the considerate phrase, "if you don't want to watch something else." Although the American guests did correctly assume that the second request would be considered more polite than the first, they grossly underestimated the acceptability of the first. The señoras seem to expect the guest to take the *initiative* in requesting things they want as long as they do it politely.

> That's the way it should be. He should say what television program he wants to see.
>
> Yes, that is companionship and if they are living in your house, they can feel perfectly free to give their opinion.
>
> As long as he asks permission and doesn't turn it on too loudly.
>
> There is always the possibility that some other member of the family may want to see another program at the same time. But occasionally it could be permitted.
>
> As long as he doesn't mind if the family says "no."
>
> If it isn't appropriate the señora would tell him, so there would be no problem.

Situation 7: The North American girl waits in her own room for the señora to come personally to invite her. The señoras' reactions to this showed clearly that this would, of course, not be considered impolite but it certainly would not be *preferred* by the host.

There is no need for that. She is like a member of the family and should make her wants known.

It is not necessary for people living in the same house to wait for someone to invite them.

It is better if she feels like a member of the family and it should be necessary to invite her only the first time.

As soon as the student arrives, I tell him to watch television whenever he wants.

The girl shouldn't wait because you never know whether she is studying or not.

You don't want to have to invite them when you don't know whether they want to watch television or not.

The host expects the guest to take the initiative in the matter. The problem is to learn how to take the initiative.

Situation 8: Would the señora think it proper for a male guest to watch T.V. with her in her room? One of the areas of doubt in the minds of both the señoras and the American guests was in the case of the male guest watching television with the señora in her bedroom. A large majority of the señoras approved the idea, but this approval depended upon important assumptions.

Only one of the señoras volunteered the information that she was aware that the male students did not watch television "because they don't dare to go to the señora's bedroom." In general they were not aware of this being a problem in the minds of the American guests. Some of the señoras merely remarked that there would be no problem because "after all, the students are just children" thus giving great weight to the generation gap as a deterrent to improper advances in either direction. Other señoras did offer qualifying conditions such as:

It depends on the boy and what the señora thinks.

It is all right unless the wife is a bride, then the husband might not like it.

It is better for another person to be present, but if only the two of them are present, it doesn't matter.

If it is in the hall or in another place, yes. But if it is in the bedroom, no!

Neutrality, Insecurity, and Noncommunication

For all of the T.V. sharing situations the American guests underestimated the number of señoras who would consider each pattern acceptable. This failure to realize the degree of approval they could expect from their hosts was *not* due to the guests' clear expectation of disapproval but because they felt *insecure* in a situation that was ambiguous to them.

A majority of the American guests had discovered the essential features of the pattern even though they did not feel sure about it. Several of the students had violated the pattern many times before they had discovered it. A sizable minority of the students had not completed this discovery process even after they had been in the home from three to six months.

In the meantime, some of the American guests developed an image of the señora as "that selfish person who monopolizes the television set." The Colombian hosts added that some Americans are aggressive or crude because they "intrude in an unacceptable manner." If guests had known the essential feature of this television sharing pattern in the *bogotano* host families, it would have reduced anxieties and prevented some of the mutually negative images between the host and the guest.

On the basis of data from both hosts and guests, we have constructed the following description of the typical pattern of television sharing. Of course all host families do not hold to every aspect of this pattern, but it seems clear that it is more accurate than a description made by any one guest or host. It would have been acceptable to the very large majority of the host families in this study. The following description deals with the cases where the television set is located in the señora's bedroom, since most sharing problems are here.

The typical sharing pattern

If joining in watching a program already in progress, the guest should always greet those already in the room before he enters. He should then either wait to be invited or directly ask if he can join them if there seems to be enough appropriate seating space. If he is invited to join the group, he should be sure there is enough seating before he accepts. "Enough seating" depends upon where this particular family is accustomed to having people sit. If there is not enough seating, he should decline politely by saying he doesn't want to crowd them.

The essential points here are that the guest (1) should first greet them, (2) obtain permission either directly or indirectly, and (3) be sensitive to whether or not he should accept the invitation on the basis of possible inconvenience to those already there.

Planning in advance to watch a T.V. program is more difficult in Colombia than in the United States. At the time of this study, no *TV Guide* published programs a week in advance. Some Sunday newspapers announce special programs in advance, and every daily paper has a television schedule for the day. Of course the guest will learn the regularly scheduled programs.

If the program is on at a later hour than the parents usually retire to the bedroom to sleep or read in bed, it is doubtful that the guest should ask to watch. Otherwise the guest should simply ask if he could see a certain television program at a specific hour if they do not already have plans to see some other program at that time.

When watching television alone, the guest should always have permission *in advance* and get instructions from the señora on using the set even though he may feel that such instruction is not necessary. It usually makes the señora feel more secure about giving permission if the guest shows a willingness to learn. If there are others in the house, the guest should not use the set beyond the hour when it is usually permitted for other family members, and the volume should not be louder than necessary.

Even though a large proportion of the señoras approved of *male guests joining the señora*, the situation should be approached with some caution because it was clear that many of the señoras were assuming that there were other members of the family at home at the time, that the señora was *not* recently married, that the male guest was much younger than the señora, and that he had established himself as being very proper (*muy correcto*) in the eyes of both the señor and the señora.

Notes

1. In the depth interviews the lack of proper greetings seemed to center around several different ideas such as: not *seeking out* family members to greet them after being away on a weekend, not taking the *initiative* in greeting visitors in the home, not taking the initiative in introducing oneself to visitors in the home, or not standing up when greeting certain types of persons on certain occasions. It is clear that these are all sins of omission and that we need to know more than we do about these patterns of greeting.
2. Edward T. Hall, *The Hidden Dimension* (Garden City, New York, Doubleday & Co., 1966), p. 128.
3. Of course this image does not spring exclusively from the guest's behavior in the bedroom, but this was part of the problem. The other facets include behavior that takes place outside the walls of the house, such as kissing the boyfriend goodnight on the front doorstep which will be described later when we deal with the topic of relations between the sexes.
4. In the case of the 26 percent who chose the negative response, we cannot be sure that it is because they had assumed certain of the restricting conditions would prevail. For example, they might have assumed we are referring to a *male* guest because their particular American guest at the moment was a male, or they might assume that there are no conditions under which they would want a guest (male or female) to come into their bedroom to use the television while they were out.

5

The Living Room and Dining Room

The Living Room

The living room (*la sala*) is not frequently a scene of serious miscommunication and conflict, perhaps because the family spends much less time downstairs. Nevertheless, there are certain problems that arose mainly because the function of *la sala* in the host household was quite different from that of the living room in the guests' own homes in the United States.

The appearance of the *sala* usually impresses the American guest as stiff and formal. It is often taboo to have a used ash tray on the coffee table or newspapers in evidence anywhere. Generally, there is no television set, no piano, no radio (unless it is in conjunction with a record player), no books, and no children's toys. It is rarely used as a gathering place for the whole family except perhaps on Sundays. Although many *salas* have a fireplace, it is not used daily even when it is chilly downstairs. The room is rarely used for long enough periods of time to warrant building a fire except on special occasions when the *sala* is used for entertaining. Also, the cost of firewood (*leña*) is much higher than in many places in the United States, and it is not burned indiscriminately during times when the room is not occupied. Too, the fastidious señora often sees the use of the fireplace as another unwelcome source of dirt in the living room.

The living room is used primarily as a gathering place for people who are not intimate friends. It is also for large parties (*fiestas bailables*) in which the record player is used, or for a cocktail party (although these are not common). It is a place for the family to present its "front" to the public in general.

Some of the host-family señoras forbid children, including teenagers, to sit on the sofa to avoid wearing it out or soiling it so that it would not be ready for company. In several of the host homes, particularly where there were small children, the living room was kept locked most of the time as insurance against being embarrassed by an untidy room if visitors came.

Another special function of the living room seems to be equivalent to that of the sitting room or parlor earlier in American history when this was the acceptable place for respectable young people to court.

The North American guests usually noticed that the living room has a function different from the United States living rooms.

> We never enter the living room here unless there is company. Otherwise it is never used. That's strictly for formal affairs. It's a very elegant room but we never use it.

> The bedrooms are upstairs and actually the only time we can use the living room is when guests come. If they are close friends they go right upstairs in the grandmother's room and that's used as a living room. Everyone sits on the bed and talks.

> The living room is not a living room the way we think of one, for living in. It is for entertaining, a special time when you have company or for a party or something like that.

> Since I have gone there, we have used the living room about five times for when they have guests. On Sundays, they open it and the whole family listens to hi-fi records. I don't think that it is a family taboo not to go into the living room; it is just that they don't think about it. They always do things in the bedroom like watch television, play games, and stuff.

> I do know that the children are forbidden to play in the living room. They have to play in their bedrooms all the time, but that's partly because it is a small house. If we had a larger house, they might have a playroom.

> The living room is kept locked. When someone comes in, the key is brought down by the maid or the señora.

> Downstairs seems to be more formal. That's where the daughter entertains her boyfriend at night. Recently, he has been coming and staying all day on Sunday. He comes in the afternoon and he is there until 9:00 at night or so. I don't think the señor approves of that, but the mother is encouraging her to get married.

The only room where a female guest could receive a male visitor was the living room except in a few cases where there was some other more specialized den or sitting room downstairs.

Despite the fact that the North American guests knew that the living room was quite a formal area, they did not appreciate the full extent of this formality. The señoras' perception of the most acceptable dress in the living room was to be completely dressed, ready for the street except for a top coat. The guests thought that the most acceptable form of dress was without jacket, sweater, or in the case of the male guests, a tie. A small minority of guests also mistakenly thought that it would be acceptable to be in pajamas, bathrobe, and slippers; in pants, shirt, and slippers, or for women, skirt, blouse, and slippers or barefooted. These forms of dress were *not* approved by any of the señoras.

There were no serious host–guest conflicts over the use of the living room area. But the guests did have to make some minor adjustments to the fact that the living room was sometimes locked, that it was supposed to be kept free of newspaper and other litter at all times, and that any family member in the living room should be dressed as if he were ready to receive company even though no company was in the house at the time. Friends visiting the home on their way upstairs would think it odd to see someone in the living room not dressed in a manner appropriate to receive company.

Occasionally a señora was shocked by the fact that the American guest would allow delivery people in the front door while he went upstairs to summon her. This is generally not acceptable for fear that something might be stolen while the guest leaves the delivery man. He expects either to wait outside the door or to deliver any item that cannot be handed to the person answering the door through the garage door. The guest should allow the maid or the señora to answer the door unless he is sure the person at the door wants to see him or the maid and señora are not in—an extremely rare occurrence.

The Dining Room

The dining room is where the family eats all three meals of the day. None of the host families had anything resembling the American breakfast nook or a common kitchen–dining room area. None of them eat meals in the kitchen. However, the behavior pattern at breakfast is very different in some ways from that at either lunch (*almuerzo*) or dinner (*comida*).

71

Breakfast

In none of the host families did the members sit down at the breakfast table at the same time. The following "scene" is an example of the type of confusion that sometimes plagued the well intentioned guest who tried to discover the appropriate time to come to breakfast.

GUEST.　Thank you, Mrs. González, for your help. I'm pretty tired from traveling so will go to bed soon. Could you tell me when you usually have breakfast?

HOST.　Just any time that you get up you can come down and have breakfast.

GUEST.　I don't want to cause you any inconvenience, I can come down any time you say.

HOST.　There is no problem, just come down any time, it really doesn't matter.

This guest was confused because he assumed that there was a certain fixed time for breakfast and that the whole family would eat together. Some guests at first assumed that the first breakfast was to be a special occasion in which the host would tolerate their coming down late if they wished to sleep. When they discovered that they were eating alone, they assumed that the whole family had eaten together earlier. So they would then ask again in a few days, "What is your customary time for breakfast?" The host would be puzzled by the guest's short memory but would give the same answer. Several of the guests when interviewed gave the same explanation of this "strange behavior of the señora."

It is almost impossible to find out when the family eats breakfast. All week I have eaten alone, but when I ask her when I should come down for breakfast . . . she just says "any time you are ready." I think that this is the Latin way of trying to please a guest. They say what they think you want to hear . . . but that makes it impossible to discover the schedule.

Sometimes, after several weeks of eating alone most of the time, a small minority of the guests began to give another interpretation to the problem.

At first I thought it was just a matter of being polite and treating me like a guest, which I didn't want to be. I want to be a regular member of the family. But I have been segregated. I don't think they want me to eat breakfast with the others. Maybe they don't dress for breakfast and think that it is too informal for me to be there with them.

Actually, this guest was being treated like a member of the family. In order to arrive at an 8:00 class he usually had to eat between 7:00 and 7:30. Many of the Colombian fathers had to leave for work by 7:00 and would have breakfast earlier downstairs or would have a "continental breakfast" in the bedroom with the señora. In other cases only the señor would eat early and the señora would have her breakfast later either upstairs or down. Then breakfast time for any children in the house would depend upon their age, whether they were in school, and the time they had to catch the bus.

In most of the homes breakfast was served over a two-hour span of time. Each member of the family came down to the dining room and the maid asked what the person wanted or simply started to serve whatever was on the menu for the day.

Sometimes confusion arose because the maid asked an American guest what he wanted for breakfast and he, not knowing the range of choices, ordered something that was not available or was very troublesome to prepare. Usually, however, the maid told the guest what the choices were; the family members already knew the possibilities. Actually the host-family breakfast closely resembled a typical breakfast in the guests' own homes in the United States. There was juice, fruit, eggs, pastry, butter or margarine, jam or jelly, and a hot beverage.

Occasionally the guest would have some difficulty with the vocabulary involved in the menu. If he had been to Mexico he would say *huevos revueltos* for scrambled eggs instead of *huevos pericos* as Colombians say. Similarly, he might say that he wants a *plátano*, hoping to get a banana to eat raw, but finds that he is given a fried banana of a different variety. In Bogotá the word *plátano* by itself is often used to denote the large variety of banana which is called *plantain* in English. It is rarely eaten raw but is usually baked, fried, or put into soup. The word *banano* refers to the ordinary variety eaten raw.

Café con leche is not simply coffee with cold milk added, but is a more concentrated form of coffee poured into the cup with *hot* milk added. In the home, one may serve himself from the two pots on the table or the maid may pour it. She will want to know when to stop pouring the coffee so that when the remainder of the cup is filled with milk it will have the right proportions to suit the taste. Sometimes confusion arises when an American says simply, "*Bastante*," when he has enough. The maid or waiter might keep pouring the coffee because he assumes that it is short for "*Quiero bastante*," (I want plenty) rather than short for "*Es bastante*." The simplest response in this situation is "Ya," when there is enough coffee.

Juice may be a mixture of orange and banana. Usually, an electric blender is used to beat the banana into the orange juice. A similar practice common in Colombia is to beat banana or any other fruit juice into milk. This is called a *sorbete*. One will find *sorbete de lulo, de guanábana, de banano, de mora*, etc. "Tropical fruit in season" may cover a number of fruits completely unfamiliar to the North American; they have no English translation. These include the *curuba, guanábana, lulo, mango, melón* (not a watermelon or cantaloupe), *papaya*, and the *pomarrosa*. Any of these plus other exotic fruits may appear from time to time on the breakfast table.

Another unfamiliar item on the breakfast menu is *arepas* which are similar to a very thin English muffin but are often flavored with cheese, butter, eggs, and milk. Also new to the American guests is *arequipe* which is a very sweet spread with an opaque caramel color. It is made of milk with sugar added and then cooked down to the consistency of honey (or thicker in some regions).

Soup may occasionally be served at breakfast, which is surprising to American guests. Americans who were accustomed to having meat such as bacon, ham, or sausage at breakfast were liable to be disappointed in the host home where meat for breakfast was a notable exception. At times or in some households a "continental breakfast" of juice, coffee, and roll may be served. There may be *sopa de pan* but no eggs because the *sopa* contains not only bread but also cheese and an egg.

The customary order of serving at breakfast would be the same as in the United States except for the tendency to serve coffee at the end of the meal.

Again, considerable lack of communication existed about the acceptable mode of dress at the breakfast table. All of the hosts thought male guests should be completely dressed ready for the street. For some reason only 40 percent of the male guests thought the señora expected this. They thought they would be overdressed.

Female guests overestimated the acceptability of the bathrobe-pajamas-slippers combinations at breakfast, but in general the degree of their misperception was not so great as the males'.

It is understandable that this communication gap should be greater regarding the norms of dress at breakfast, where the guest is usually eating alone, than at lunch or dinner when the family eats together and the guest has an opportunity to observe.

Lunchtime *(almuerzo)*

The word for the noon meal differs in Latin American countries. For example, in Mexico *la comida* is most popular, and in Bogotá *el almuerzo* is standard. In the verb forms, *almorzar* means to eat lunch, and *comer* often means specifically to eat dinner, rather than to eat in general.[1]

Lunchtime is generally between 12:30 and 1:30 and ends between 1:30 and 2:45. The most popular lunch period is between 1:00 and 2:00 p.m. Lunch is a more formal occasion than breakfast, and the whole family is more likely to eat together than at either breakfast or dinner.

The host family señor nearly always comes home for lunch even though he works downtown. This is the best opportunity for him to spend time with his young children since they might go to bed before he returns at night. The *almuerzo* is an important family time. Some of the guests who did not eat lunch in their host home got the impression that the family was rarely together since they did not realize the husband would brave the noontime traffic to come home for lunch.

The señoras expected the guests to let them know if they were unable to come to lunch or dinner on time. In some cases if the guest wanted to go to a 6:00 movie (*vespertina*), he could call the señora to say that he would miss *comida*, and she would arrange with the maid to keep some food warm for when he returned. The guest was expected to minimize the number of emergencies by planning ahead and telling the señora when leaving in the morning if he expected to miss a meal.

The Menu

The typical lunch menu in the host families was more exotic to the American guest than the breakfast menu. There is little difference between the items that might appear at lunch and dinner. A typical menu for either meal follows overleaf.

Menu A lists the most popular items, menu B the second, and C the third. These three menus might account for about 60 to 75 percent of the meals served, while the remainder of the meals included a much wider variety of foods that are not served so regularly. Most foods that are strange to the North American guest are not included in the three "standard menus," but are among those served less frequently. The names of these foods are less likely to have an English translation.

All 14 categories of foods are not served at every *almuerzo* and *comida*. Although soup is not served at every meal, the frequency and variety of soups is greater than customary in the United States. Some types of soup, for example *sopa de pan*, are used as the main dish. It contains bread, cheese, and eggs among other ingredients and is quite heavy and nourishing. Sometimes fruit or cheese is served in place of a dessert. Sometimes bread is not served because there is either *pasta* or rice, or both.

An impression of the majority of the American guests was that there was generally *less variety* in the meal, not only in that the *comida* might strongly resemble the *almuerzo* in the same day, but also certain items reappeared very frequently throughout the month or year. This impression may be partly based upon an objective difference in the amount of variety to which the American is accustomed, but also if certain of the frequently

Table 1. Typical Lunch and Dinner Menu in Colombian Host Homes

	BEVERAGES	SOUPS	FRUITS	MEATS	STARCHES
(A)	*Café negro* (coffee)	*Arroz y papa* (rice & potato)	*Banano* (banana)	*Lomito de res* (steak)	*Pan* (rolls)
(B)	*Café con leche* (coffee with milk)	*Plátano* (plantain)	*Piña* (pineapple)	*Carne asada* (roast beef)	*Spaguetti* (spaghetti)
(C)	*Leche* (milk)	*Verduras* (vegetable)	*Papaya* (papaya)	*Hígado* (liver) *Pollo* (chicken)	*Macarrones* (macaroni) *Yuca* (?)

	COOKED VEGETABLE	RAW VEGETABLE	CONDIMENTS	SPREADS	DESSERTS
(A)	*Arroz* (rice)	*Tomates* (tomatoes)	*Salsa de tomate* (ketchup)	*Mantequilla o margarina* (butter or margarine)	*Gelatina* (jello)
(B)	*Papas* (potatoes)	*Lechuga* (lettuce)	*Salsa Picante* (hot sauce)	*Mermelada* (jam or jelly)	*Galletas* (cookies)
(C)	*Plátano* (plantain)	*Cocombro* (cucumber)	*Vinagre y aceite* (vinegar and oil)	*Arequipe* (arequipe)	*Bizcochos* (pastries)

	JUICES	EGG DISHES	SEA FOODS	OTHER	
(A)	*Guayaba* (guava)	*Con arroz y carne* (with rice and meat)	*Camarón* (shrimp)	*Queso* (cheese)	
(B)	*Piña* (pineapple)	*Fritos* (fried)	*Robalo* (haddock)	*Empanadas* (empanadas)	
(C)	*Papaya* (papaya)	*Pericos* (with onions and tomato)	*Bagre* (river fish)	*Yogurt* (yogurt)	

reappearing foods are not liked because they are strange, their re-appearance seems all the more monotonous. However, the guests observed that there was a wide variety of soups, fruit, and juices.

There is less meat in the Colombian menu than in the United States. This puzzles American guests when they learn that beef is cheap in comparison to the price in the States. However, it is higher in relation to the average middle-class *bogotano* income.

Most American guests, particularly those who had lived in smaller towns in Mexico, were quite surprised at the lack of spicy, *picante* foods. In fact, about one-third of the students felt that there was less seasoning in the food than in the United States. Usually when a hot sauce is used, it is in a separate dish so that each individual may use as much or as little as he pleases.

Another general impression of the guests was that sometimes the breakfast was smaller and the *almuerzo* was larger than in the United States, and the señora expected them to eat more than they often wanted. However, the American admitted that he probably would have eaten more if he had been allowed to follow his usual habit of snacking whenever he wished in the afternoon or late at night. But this is *not* the pattern in Colombia and would bring the guest into conflict with the maid or señora. In some cases, the guest was shocked to find the refrigerator locked.

It has often been said that one of the most powerful bases of patriotism is gastronomic. If other people eat what we consider inedible, we consider them peculiar in their tastes. Even when we are intellectually able to concede their sovereign right to eat what they please, we may not be so open minded when we have to eat at their table; One's own stomach also wishes to assert its right.

Without doubt, the dimension of diet that caused the most culture shock to students and Peace Corps trainees was the amount of starch.

The biggest problem that we have is the food. There has been absolutely no variety, and we can see no reason for it. They are a middle-class family and can afford to give us some variety even if it is only eggs for breakfast.

I made a joke about only having *arroz, arroz, arroz*. The señora misunderstood, was hurt and mad, and said that if I wanted I could leave. That has been straightened out, though.

I was used to eating very small amounts of starches in the United States. Here I always have rice, potatoes, and some sort of soup with potatoes or *plátano* in it. Then sometimes we will have fried bananas in addition.

I have difficulty in making a respectable dent in the starch pile. There is so much rice, potatoes, noodles, *yuca* . . . and it is always there.

There is always rice for lunch and dinner, many more potatoes than in the United States, and *yuca* keeps popping up all the time. The rice and potatoes are very hard [not cooked long enough].

The vegetables, with the exception of *yuca*, rice, and potatoes, are rarely served individually, but in a sort of mush which appears on a separate plate with rice . . . about half rice and half mush.

Gastronomic culture shock

Often an American guest arrived in Colombia determined to follow dietary customs. He had fantasies of eating unusual foods such as squid, goat, fried grasshoppers, fried maguey worms, or foods smoldering with chili pepper. Some of these ideas were obtained from looking at the gourmet shelf in the local super market in the United States; some he derived from tales of North Americans who have been to Mexico. He was usually not prepared for what he found. Instead of the mysterious and exotic he found that the food is very "bland," "starchy," "greasy," and "monotonous." The gastronomic jolt was not in specific strange foods but in a different *balance* of fairly familiar items.

The Colombian gets his carbohydrates mainly in starches, while the North American prefers a larger proportion in the form of sugar in jello, cookies, jam, jelly, honey, syrup, cake, pie, and canned fruits. Even when a person wants starch, he wants it in the form to which he is accustomed. Many guests found it difficult to believe that the Colombian family would really miss *yuca*, which often seemed tasteless to the North Americans. The guests' objections to specific items in the diet reflected not only their general North American middle-class backgrounds, but in some cases they reflected particular subcultures.

There are no grits for breakfast.
We have never had any hominy grits.
There are no lox and bagels on Sunday morning!
A little piece of pickled herring would be nice.

The gastronomic disturbance of the North American guest is not merely a physiological problem nor a private problem of the guest. It tends to become a disturbing factor in the relationships between guest and host. Even though all the organizations sponsoring the American guests had the policy that the American should not expect any special dietary consideration in the host home, and even though most guests were striving to accommodate, most of the señoras were sharply aware that the food was a problem for their guests and hence for themselves.

We have to worry about food because some things she may not like but we can't afford to give a lot of special food. Usually we try to make the food the American way so the change will not be so hard for the student, but we worry about it and the students worry about it. The main problem I think is food.

Karen would taste everything but Sue didn't. I would tell Karen, "Try everything, and if you don't like it you don't have to eat it!" and she wouldn't. She thought that *guama* (fruit) looked like cotton or wool and she hesitated to eat it. But I urged her to try it and she liked it very much.

I never prepared anything special for the students, but I would buy special things. For example, they told me they didn't like the desserts so I used to buy cookies for them.

Ned was difficult with food. He didn't like anything! He said he didn't want to say he liked something special because we might serve it to him every day. [This was a complaint of some of the guests.] Anyway I'd tell him that I would prefer that he would be frank and say if he *didn't* like something. The menu was very limited because he liked so few things.

I told Robert that he didn't like anything and he said, "That's right," and when you hear that they don't like any of the food you try less. You stop going to the kitchen to make special food because they are not going to eat it anyway.

Of course we have Colombian food, but the students love it. They love fruit, and they even eat *yuca* and *plátano* at times. They never expect me to make special food for them.

Sometimes I would give my children an egg and sometimes I would not. I would tell my children I wasn't giving them one because they could eat the other things, so my children began to ask, "Mother, why do you have to feed him special things and not us?" I said, "Because I feel embarrassed that he will go hungry." They'd say "Force him to eat because the program says he should eat everything," and I should have done it. I think I made a big mistake. I guess it was a maternal instinct even though he was not my own son. I felt sorry that he would not eat, very sorry, and I'd say, "Well, poor boy . . . maybe he will suffer," and also I was a little proud. I had a pride that people shouldn't think that he was not fed enough in my house!

Not only were many of the señoras aware that the food was a problem for the guest but if he was not pleased with the food, they felt it a reflection upon their pride and reputation. Some hosts found it impossible to accept this apparent rejection of their food as a symptom of culture shock rather than as a personal rejection. Other hosts realized that there would inevitably be certain dishes the guest would not like because they were different, but they found it difficult to accept the idea that the guest might not even taste the food or that he did so but failed to learn to like it.

The guests seemed to resist milk most. This seemed to be a source of constant amazement to the señora.

Becky would have lots of coffee, but I forced her to have some milk in it. They have been told that the milk here was very bad, but I told them the milk here was very good. They brought the milk to me from a farm where it was good. At first she would drink it only in coffee but later she would drink it alone.

At these lectures they had in the United States they are advised not to drink milk. I'd insist that she drink milk because she was very thin. I'd tell her that it wasn't true that the cows have tuberculosis. I think they are sick in their mind because they eat the meat and never worry.

The American guests heard rumors, mainly in the American community, that the milk was not pasteurized even when it said so on the label. They heard that during the dry season when milk was not plentiful, the distributors would illegally add water instead of raising the price since the prices are fixed by government regulation. They heard rumors about tests that showed the presence of many kinds of germs that would have been eliminated by a correct pasteurization. They did not know whether boiling the milk in the home would eliminate the danger, and they didn't know whether their families boiled the milk and felt it would be impolite to ask.

When the guest knew that the milk was boiled routinely in the home, he encountered another barrier when he found he did not like the taste of the milk. After milk is boiled, the flavor changes. It may also have a different proportion of cream than that in the States. The milk comes from a different breed of cows and their diet is different, and in Colombia it is often not served so cold as American milk. These physical differences in the milk had greater psychological significance because the guest was worried about catching a disease from the milk.

Among the guests who resolved this dilemma and reduced the tension very quickly in a way that seemed acceptable to the host was the following:

I told the señora that I was supposed to drink only boiled milk, and she said that she always had it boiled anyway as soon as it came into the house. I also told her that I was not in the habit of drinking much milk alone but liked it in *café con leche* and in *sorbetes*. I can actually stand the taste of milk straight if I have to, but it is better if it is mixed with something else.

Even though most of the guests tried to adjust to the Colombian diet and did not voice any of their dislikes, the hosts had a fairly accurate idea of some of the guests' food aversions but were ignorant of others.

The hosts' disagreement with the idea that their guests "don't like Colombian food" was well founded. The Americans did like much of it and found certain items such as the fruits, juices, and soups better than at home. In general the hosts agreed that their guests didn't like so many starches and were correctly aware of the guests' love of raw salads, fresh fruits, and the variety of Colombian soups. The two negative reactions of American guests not realized by the majority of the hosts were the lack of variety and the abundance of oil in the cooking. Apparently the guests managed to keep these dislikes hidden from the señora.

Cultural differences in food tastes caused considerable strain in cross-cultural communication. The Americans who did not like certain dishes did not want to insult the hosts by not eating them. Yet it did him little good to eat stoically or feign delight because the reward for his diplomatic stoicism was being served more of the same. He could eat a token amount, leave it all without any remarks, say that he was not hungry, or straightforwardly say that he didn't like a certain dish.

It was difficult to find a way to do any of these and avoid hurting the señora's feelings. Often it was the señoras who had been voluntarily making a special effort to please the guest who felt most rejected when they realized their efforts were in vain. The señora would often mistakenly assume that the guest realized that he was being given special consideration, but he actually had no way of knowing how the food was ordinarily served.

The señora interpreted his behavior to indicate the guest was ungrateful or that he took this special care for granted because he felt he was superior. The guest who neglected to make comments about positive aspects of the food did not build up his stock with the señora so that he could refuse a dish occasionally without giving the impression "He doesn't like my food."

Some of the Americans made the false assumption that since the señora did not actually do the cooking, her ego would not suffer if the guest did not like the food. Since his own mother in the States did not have a maid or cook, he did not realize the degree to which the maid was an extension of the señora's ego.

Many of the guests did not realize how much they nonverbally communicated their dislike for a certain food. They assumed that if they said nothing they would insult no one. Yet the señora might be acutely aware of the fact. When the guest assumed that the señora was not aware of his rejection of the food, he made no special effort to counterbalance the effect.

Fear of contamination

The guest sometimes rejected certain foods because of his fear of contamination. In addition to worrying about the effects of milk consumption, he was anxious about the water, the vegetables, and insects.

Although most of the guests mentioned that they took considerable pains to hide their anxieties and avoid embarrassing the host, the hosts were nevertheless aware of them.

She was frightened about getting contaminated and she had special pills to put in the water and other pills to put in vegetables. She didn't use them in the house, but she was afraid of getting contaminated. It was too exaggerated. I knew she was doing it because the maid told me. Maybe she opened the closet because she told me she saw special pills for amoebas. And when they have these lectures in the United States they advise them not to drink the water.

One thing they are afraid of is vegetables because they say that they might get a lot of amoebas. I have tried to fight the idea to get them not to believe this. I have told them that we wash the vegetables and that here in the house there is cleanliness in the kitchen and that we cook them previously and that we put in lime juice so that they won't get amoebas. So I have tried to fight the idea and I give them vegetables.

A majority of the hosts were aware of the guests' general fear of catching diseases; drinking the milk; and flies, fleas, and mosquitos. Almost half felt that they were also fearful of drinking the water.

Most of the Americans drank some milk after they discovered that the family did boil it, and many simply broke their habit of drinking water with meals and drank juice, coffee, *café con leche*, or *gaseosas* instead. But in the meantime they directly or indirectly communicated their anxieties.

Even though a guest would guard his remarks about the food most of the time, he would sometimes spontaneously follow his impulse as shown in the following dialogue.

HOST. Do you eat avocados in the United States?
GUEST. Yes, we have lots of them there too.
HOST. But you have not learned to like them.
GUEST. Yes, I like them very much!
HOST. But I have never seen you eat any here.
GUEST. Is it safe to eat them when they are raw? I usually try not to eat any raw vegetables!
HOST. Oh yes, it is perfectly safe. They have been washed in FAB (detergent) before they were peeled!

Often upon reflection, the American is embarrassed when he realizes how thoughtless it is to ask if a food is safe to eat when it is on the table and the host is obviously eating it. Among the logical assumptions that could justify such a question are that the host is immune to whatever danger lurks, the host served the food to the guest with no intention of eating any himself, or the host does not care about his own health and is perfectly willing to eat unsafe food. Of course the guest is not actually basing his question on any of these assumptions or being logical. He is simply verbalizing his anxiety.

However, the danger to the interpersonal relations is that the host sometimes felt that the guest's question was based on one of the assumptions and highly resented its implications. Others were only amused by the guest's spontaneous expression of his anxieties or by his youthfully innocent approach. It is understandable, however, that if a particular guest has manifested an attitude of superiority in other ways, it would be easy for the host to think, "Here he goes again! He thinks the food we feel is good enough for us is not good enough for him!" Only on rare occasions did a señora directly verbalize this feeling.

> She would not eat the salads; she would not drink the milk; and when she caught a cold, she refused to drink *agua de panela* with *limón* but took her own pills. When I offered to call a doctor, she wouldn't let me because she thought I wouldn't know a good doctor. Then one day she asked if it was alright to eat the lettuce on the hamburger I had made especially for her...so I said, "If you are afraid to eat food in my house, then you should have them change you to some house you might trust!" She was embarrassed and so was I, but after that she quit complaining about the food.

This was an extreme case both in the amount of anxiety expressed by the guest and in the overt reaction of the host, but it is symbolic of a fairly wide and pervasive undercurrent in the guest–host relationship.

Substituting foods

Another dimension of food-related tension was over the guest's direct or indirect attempt to obtain special foods. Often since the guest did not ask for it, he may not have realized that the host had already been trying to provide special foods in order to get him to eat. Also, when he did show some special preferences, he might not have known that he was increasing the host's expenditure for food to a considerable extent. The following excerpts from interviews with the señoras illustrate some of the ways in which the Americans gave the impression that they expected the best.

> We knew that Americans like pie, so we made some pineapple pie but he didn't seem to like that very well. He thought that apple pie was the best.

> We really can't afford to serve special foods for the Americans even when we know that they are not enthusiastic about the Colombian food.

> One of the girls in my mother-in-law's house wanted grapes, pears, apples, salami, and such expensive foods and showed no concern over the high price of these things.

> In some houses the situation must be terrible where they feel, *"Llegó la gringa, pongan la fruta!"* (Here comes the American, put on the fruit!), implying a demand for special foods.

The American guest might have assumed that canned fruit is relatively inexpensive since so many fresh fruits are inexpensive, but this was not true. It was not unusual for a can of peaches to cost $1.25. Fresh apples cost at least $1.00 per pound; grapes were as high as $0.75 per pound. If the American had known this, he probably would have "preferred" *mangos* which were actually very inexpensive, even though some of the Americans still thought of them as an exotic gourmet item available only in a delicatessen.

Similarly, the Americans who discovered that the price of steaks in a restaurant is lower than in the United States, often did not understand that this was still a high price to the Colombian middle-class family of five who might have an annual income of $4,500 per year.

The Peace Corps trainees were shocked to find that a married couple in the Peace Corps in Colombia often had a higher combined income than the middle-class family with four children with whom they lived during their training period.[2] They thought of themselves as sacrificing a considerable amount, and they were correct in assuming that their income could have been doubled had they stayed in the United States. Thus, we have a basic dilemma: The individual from the richer nation is making a considerable financial sacrifice but this is not perceived as such by the person from a poorer nation.

Once the American guest was aware of the cost of foods in terms of the local salaries, sometimes he would still insist that this was not relevant in view of the fact that he was paying 800 pesos ($49.05) per month for board and room. He seemed to feel that all of this amount should go into food and did not allow for added cost of bottled gas for hot showers, an extra item of furniture (e.g., a reading lamp), extra work for the maid, and his room. Even in the majority of cases where the guest was aware of the different kinds of additional expenses incurred by the host in having an American guest, there was a marked lack of awareness of the fact that even if the señora were willing to obtain some special food items craved by the American guest—such as mayonnaise, cold meats, or canned fruits —it would be either a problem for her if she didn't offer the same foods to all members of the family, or it would be a financial problem if she did. Some of the little extras which might amount to only $6.00 per month additional for the American would amount to $30 to $35 per month if offered to all members of the family. None of the Americans interviewed showed a clear recognition of this dilemma. Although he might have the same problem empathizing with his own mother in the United States, there is considerable evidence that cross-cultural empathy is a more difficult feat. If nothing else, the sheer gastronomic culture shock tends to interfere with both empathy and logic.

Permissible dress at the dinner table

One striking overall pattern was the great difference between what was permissible dress at breakfast and what was permissible at lunch or dinner. Dress was more formal, and this difference was greater than the guests suspected.

To point out one of the greatest gaps in communication, none of the Colombian hosts thought that any combination of bathrobe, pajamas, and slippers was permissible, while 31 percent of the female guests did not realize this. Only 69 percent of the female guests felt it would be appropriate to be completely dressed ready for the street when eating lunch. All of the female guests thought it permissible to eat lunch without jacket or sweater, while only 89 percent of the señoras felt this way. Since they had all eaten lunch with the family many times and since the señora was nearly always present, we could speculate that there are several possible explanations for this gap in communication: The female guests failed to observe that the señora *did* wear her jacket; the señora did not wear a jacket or sweater but thought the younger female guest should do so; the señora had a nostalgic allegiance to the idea of wearing the jacket or sweater which was an ideal no longer put into practice; the guest did observe that the señora wore her jacket or sweater, but the guest assumed that because she was younger she was not expected to dress like the señora.

The male guests had no single mode of dress they all thought would be acceptable to the señora. Also, the male guests underestimated the preference for the most formal mode of dress even more than the female guests. This is probably because about one-third of the male guests lived in homes where the father was not present, so he had no model to follow. Possibly the male guests thought that even though their Colombian father did wear his jacket at the dinner table, this was only a symbol of his age, dignity, or status not to be copied by a younger person. None of the male guests thought robe, pajamas, and slippers were acceptable.

Guests should dress in the most conservative manner to be acceptable to all the señoras. In families where there is no son or a daughter the same age as the guest, he could not determine from direct observation whether the expected mode of dress was the same for parent and child. This could be discovered by asking the señora, "If you had a daughter my age, would you expect her to wear a sweater or jacket at lunch?"

The trend toward hippy dress and grooming in the United States increased the culture gap between the North Americans and the Latin Americans. However, most of the North Americans made a decided effort to change their mode of dress at least to some degree in the direction of the host-family standards. This adjustment varied not only for individual Americans but according to the particular United States college campus he came from. For example, the students from Hope College (a Dutch Reformed Church School) had little difficulty making the adjustment, while the average student from Antioch College had to adapt much more to bridge the gap.

It was difficult for the American to believe that only a few years ago standards of dress in Bogotá were even more formal. For example, only five years earlier, I recall seeing bulldozer operators wearing regular dress suits, white shirt, and tie. Graduate students in physics at Javeriana University, while building electronic equipment, manipulated their soldering irons with finesse while dressed in a suit, white shirt, cuff links, vest, and jacket. No apron, coveralls, or other protective clothing was worn. Although the dress on university campuses in Bogotá has changed very markedly toward less formality, the trend in the United States is such that the contrast has not been eliminated.

Informal dress of the American student would be considered "rural" by the Colombian (rather than "intellectual" as in the United States student culture). Sometimes this impression was strengthened by the American wearing a *ruana* of the type found only in the rural areas of Colombia. American tourists, students, and Peace Corps trainees often did this, thinking they were identifying with Colombians but did not distinguish between different types of *ruanas*.

The failure of the American guest to either discover or to conform to the Colombians' expectations with regard to dress both inside and outside the home resulted in negative images of the Americans in a considerable proportion of Colombian hosts. For example, 55 percent of the hosts felt that their guests did not dress appropriately for the circumstances, 51 percent felt that they "dress more like farmers than like city people," and 39 percent felt that their guests were "messy in personal appearance."

Notes

1. This is a cause of confusion when a Colombian asks an American, *"Ya ha comido usted hoy?"* depending upon the time of day the question is asked. It is most confusing to the American if asked between 8:00 and 9:00 p.m., which could be either before or after dinner. So while the Colombian is asking specifically if he has had dinner today, the American might think he is simply asking if he has eaten today. The correct answer to the Colombian might be "No" but he says "Yes" since he has eaten two meals already.

2. A Peace Corps volunteer couple jointly received a living allowance of 3,300 pesos per month (equal to $2,437 per year) plus $75 per month which was held for them in the United States ($1,800 per year)—a total yearly income of $4,227—plus certain fringe benefits such as medical services, travel, and insurance.

   Some full-time Colombian professors with four children, working at the National University, had a salary equivalent to $3,600 per year.

II

Role Relationships of the American Guest in the Colombian Home

6

The Expectation-
Realization Gap

When I talked with the American guests in the United States before they left for Colombia and later interviewed them after they had lived in the Colombian home for some weeks, it was apparent that the Americans had certain unconscious expectations regarding their role in the Colombian family and the role relationships between the members of the family. There was often a considerable gap between their expectations and the realities they found. These false expectations were sometimes the source of disappointment, confusion and miscommunication.

The nature of the expectation gap experienced by a particular American often depended upon the type of Colombian family he wanted to live with: the age, sex and number of children, and the age, social class, and educational background of the parents. If the American was not placed with the type of family he had envisioned, he tended to blame the sponsoring organization for any of the problems he had in getting along in the Colombian home. If he was placed in the type of family he had requested, he still found about the same amount of problems in adjusting. In both cases a large gap existed between the guest's expectations and the cultural reality in which he later found himself. Often he wanted conditions that were mutually exclusive in the *bogotano* culture. In fact some of the expectations would have also been impossible to attain at home in the United States.

In talking with students and Peace Corps trainees both before they left the States and after they had been placed with *bogotano* families, it became clear that some of the complaints they were voicing were due to unrealistic, conflicting, and sometimes ethnocentric expectations regarding family life in Colombia in general and their role as guests in particular.

"I don't want to live with a rich family because I want to get to know the average Colombian." Somehow this statement has an acceptable democratic ring to it on a campus in the United States. The American who says this often has an unconscious assumption that the "average" family in Colombia somehow resembles the socioeconomic average in the United States. It is clearly unrealistic to expect the average American college student to live with the average Colombian family which has a per capita income of under $500 per year. The average family is a "lower-class" family speaking either socially or economically, yet the same student who wants to live with a lower-class family in Colombia actually avoids association with lower-class North American families.

A special effort was made by CEUCA to place the Peace Corps trainees with lower-middle-class families as a step in the direction of the lower-class rural families in villages where they were going to work on various community development projects. The trainees' main source of irritation was due to the lack of physical comforts associated with low income living. These "complaints" fell mainly into 12 types, and they were strongly related to a lack of affluence of either the particular family or of the economy of the country in general.

Although the trainees were asked to mention what was different not only what was unpleasant, all but two of the 123 differences mentioned were things that were considered negative.[1] When some of the trainees asked how to interpret the word *different* in the question, they were told to "think of anything that surprised them, pleasantly or unpleasantly, anything which required new behavior patterns on their part, or anything they felt they had to adjust to, or just found different."

The predominantly negative reactions are due to several general factors. First, since the trainees come from a more affluent society, they are aware of the relative deprivations, which of course, are accompanied by negative feelings. Second, it generally takes longer to become aware of or to be able to take advantage of the positive aspects of the situation—for example, the freedom to have breakfast at any time between 6:30 and 9:00 a.m. or to have coffee or orange juice in bed in the morning or to be free of the hot dry air indoors in the winter time or to have the home quiet for studying up to 5:30 p.m. in spite of the fact that there are four children between the ages of 7 and 14. They rarely saw these things as opportunities. Third, there is a strong tendency to take the advantages for granted, particularly the freedoms, because the quest for freedom is often an important conscious or unconscious motivation for going abroad; so the freedoms are expected or even demanded. Fourth, many do not make a fair comparison with the States because they are not comparing the situation of being a guest in a home in the States with their situation in Colombia. Instead, they unwittingly combine the pleasant aspects of living in their own home with those of living in a college dormitory in the States, then compare these with being a guest in a private home in Colombia.

Some Americans living with a middle-class family object that "they don't have a variety of good food which they certainly could afford," yet they sometimes feel that the family has upper-class "aristocratic and undemocratic" attitudes and beliefs. Basically, he forgets that "middle class" is always relative to some particular economic, social, and cultural system, and he should not expect the middle class in New York to be at the same economic level as the middle class in Bogotá. Nor should he expect the style of life, values, or beliefs to be the same. If he does, he is bound to be jolted when he arrives at the moment of truth.

"I don't want to live with a family where they take house guests because they are interested in my money!" The "average" Colombian would certainly need the money. If the American knew something about the finances of many of the middle-class families, he would agree that they too need the money. The "average" family, or even the lower-middle-class family, would be less likely to have other motivations such as learning English, getting to know a foreigner, or making contact with an American. A minority of the families are motivated mainly by an altruistic concern with improving international or cross-cultural relations, and it would be surprising if an "average" family with only some primary school education were vitally interested in international problems. Even where this altruistic motivation is strong enough to accept a foreign house guest for a few days or weeks, it is another matter to accept a guest for several months or a year![2]

If the American does not want to live with a family who wants his money, then what does he feel he has to offer the host family in exchange for the trouble and expense? Some Americans ethnocentrically assumed that the Colombian would be fascinated with him and that there would be a large demand for American student guests.

This attitude of innocent self-confidence was manifested by some students who in recruitment meetings in the United States would say:

> I would like a list of the families who want Americans and some information about each one so that I can pick out the one I would like.
>
> I would like a family with a college-age daughter.
>
> Can I get a family with a piano so that I can practice?
>
> I would like a family who is politically radical.
>
> Could I pick out two or three families to write to a few months in advance so that I can pick the one that has some of the same interests I have?
>
> I would prefer a family who has never had an American before.
>
> The more cosmopolitan family with international interests, where the mother is the intellectual type, would be the best for me.

All of these statements and questions imply certain assumptions. The main assumption seems to be that there is an unlimited supply of Colombian host families for American guests, that it is possible to have a firm list of families many months in advance, and that the American guest is the one who should make the choice. An opposite set of assumptions is closer to reality: that the supply of potential host families is limited at any one point in time, that it is impossible to obtain firm commitments months in advance (some families change their mind about having a guest during the 48 hours before the American arrives), that some of the host families will take a guest only under certain conditions, that those who have never had an American guest before have doubts and fears regarding the experience, that many of those who have had the experience do not care to repeat it even in cases where the guest was one of the best, and that some families who had a particularly problematical guest give notice that they will never do it again.

Even in those cases where the guest does obtain a host family with the characteristics he wants, his expectations of this family may contradict each other or may be contrary to other realities that exist in that type of family in Colombia. This is shown in the next case where the American specifies the composition of the family he would like to live with.

"I want to live with a family that has a son or daughter my age." Fortunately, this desire is not universal because it often has some built-in dilemmas. For example, the guest may not want to live with a family in the top economic bracket, yet a middle-class family is much less likely to have extra space for a guest unless at least some of the children, most likely the college-aged ones, have left the home. Also, a señora who has reached the age when all of her children have gone, often ventures into taking an American guest because she feels lonely.

The transition to this loneliness for the *bogotana* can be more sudden than for her North American counterpart for two reasons: The children, particularly the girls, stay in the home a larger portion of the time until they are married; it is more difficult for the Colombian señora to find a variety of activities and freedom of movement outside the home or to find a remunerative job after her children have grown. One compensatory factor in favor of the *bogotana* is that her married children visit her more frequently than in a North American middle-class family. Nevertheless, this need for companionship was demonstrated in two ways. Since it is the señora rather than the señor who is most restricted to the home, it is she who wants the guest and decides to take a guest. We know from the case materials that the señora usually prefers a female guest who will provide more companionship.

These reasons reduce the probability of the American's finding families with a son or daughter his own age. Of course, there are middle-class families in which only the oldest child has left, thus providing space. However, other children who had been doubling up in one bedroom often now want to spread out. Even so, the mere availability of space does not necessarily generate the desire to have a long-term house guest when there are still children at home.

The desire of the señora to earn some extra money is the most prevalent motivation. Of course the señora could also earn extra money by taking a *Colombian* student boarder, but the second most prevalent motivation is to practice English.

Here we have another dilemma. The guest is in Colombia to learn Spanish, and the host often would like an American guest in order to practice English. However, the "desire to learn English" was usually restricted to the host's occasionally asking the guest the meaning of a word in something he was reading or how to pronounce a word in English. In other cases the guest and host arrived at an agreement that at certain times the host would speak English while the guest continued to respond in Spanish, each correcting the other's errors. This had the value of generating mutual empathy for each other's linguistic problems while providing some systematic assistance.

When the American wants a family with a "son or daughter my own age" he often has in mind one of the opposite sex. This is not very likely to happen in the *bogotano* culture. There is a clear tendency for the Colombian señora to avoid having a guest of the same age and opposite sex as one of her own children. In the few cases where they did not avoid it, they had difficulty with the developing sexual attraction between their daughter and the male guest.

When the American guest obtained his wish to live with a family with an offspring of the same age and sex, the guest was sometimes disappointed because he had unconsciously assumed that he would be close friends with the Colombian. He had fantasies of spending a lot of time together, just the two of them. This is obviously unrealistic unless we assume that either the Colombian had been a social outcast awaiting the arrival of the American guest or that he was willing to forsake his former friends to spend most of his prime social time with the foreigner. The only way the American can be friends with the Colombian is to accept and participate with the Colombian's friends in a way which is acceptable to these friends.

The female American guest in some cases had a dream of living with a Colombian family with a daughter her own age who would obligingly introduce her to many interesting Colombian males. This rarely happened. Sometimes it happened at first until the Colombian girl discovered that the *gringa* has many "unfair advantages" vis-à-vis the *colombianos*: She is interesting because she is exotic, the Colombian boys think that she is sexually free, or she does not accept as many of the family's supervisory restrictions as does the Colombian daughter.

The *gringa* may behave in a way that embarrasses the Colombian daughter who then ceases to assume the liability of having her own reputation damaged by reflection. In other cases the Colombian daughter ceases to help the *gringa* because she feels that the competition is already stiff enough.

From the point of view of the Colombian señora, another type of problem may develop when there is a daughter approximately the same age as the *gringa*: The *gringa*, who has been accustomed to less parental supervision and restriction on her movements even at home and still less when abroad, will set a bad example for the Colombian daughter. In these cases a social wedge is driven by the *gringa* between the mother and her daughter because the daughter resents the *gringa* having freedoms she herself is not allowed to enjoy; she pressures her mother for similar freedoms. The mother feels that the *gringa's* bad example makes it difficult to control her own child for the protection of the child and the reputation of the mother.

This concept of the guest as a "wedge" between mother and child is not restricted to the role of the female guest but was also found in some of the families with male guests. This interaction pattern is so important in the cross-cultural relations between host and guest that a special section will be devoted to it later.

"I want to live with a family having small children." It is usually the

gringa who expresses this desire to live with a family with small children. Many reasons are given for this.

I just like children.

I'm studying to be a teacher, and I would like to see how they bring up their children in Colombia.

If the children are younger, it is just a younger and more modern family who would understand the younger generation of Americans a little better.

Of course all of these are potential advantages that were realized in some cases. To counterbalance these advantages, there are also some potential disadvantages unique to this type of host family that are rarely anticipated by the enthusiastic would-be guest.

The college-aged guest soon realizes that he had forgotten how much noise young children make. There are not only the delighted giggles and shrieks of the children but also the shouts of the irate mother and the crying of the children. In addition, children are curious and frequently invade the guest's room, his closet, and his chest of drawers to examine such interesting things as cameras, unusual articles of clothing, and other personal belongings. Often the guest is at a loss as to how to handle the child who is becoming increasingly exasperating. In several cases the guests admitted finally having to spank, scold, or lock out the invading child. He feels guilty because his action seems incompatible with his role as guest in the house. But as one *gringo* said with some defensiveness:

They told me that I was a regular member of the family and that I should treat him like my own little brother. So I did exactly that, I had told him twice that if he did it again I would spank him and when I did it he was too amazed to cry . . . but he never did it again and I'm much happier about the whole situation!

The guest can unwittingly drive a wedge between parent and child even when the child is only 10 or 12 years old. Here instead of the guest providing a bad example for the child himself to follow, the guest provides an example to the child of how the father should behave. The typical problem is one in which the American guest with the best of intentions gives candy to the child, takes him out for a hamburger or to a movie. The American is usually surprised when he detects some uneasiness, particularly in the father. In a few cases the father flatly refused to allow the child to go to a movie with the *gringo*. The father may fear that during the months the guest is in the home the child may become "spoiled" by having his level of expectations raised beyond the level the father can provide after the guest has gone. These invitations often occur on weekends which is the major opportunity for the father to be together with his children. In effect, the *gringo* is unwittingly usurping the father's role. This is not to say that it is always undesirable to take the children to a movie as a way of reciprocating for some of the favors received from the family, but that it should be clearly a special occasion, not a habit, and should have the blessing of the parents.

A third potential problem of the college-aged guest in the young family is in the relationship between the guest and the parent of the opposite sex. It was noted that in cases where the couple was young, the guest was female, and the wife was going out of town for two or three weeks to visit her parents while her husband remained in Bogotá, the wife insisted on moving the *gringa* to a friend's home for this period.

Notes

1. The two positive responses were "The house is very neat and tidy," and "The family is less prying into my personal affairs than my real family!"
2. This point was brought home forcefully when I was trying to find host homes, in a town of 4,500 population in the United States, for two Colombian secretaries. This intellectual college town had been willing to house up to 50 foreign students on very short notice up to a period of a week, but it was much more difficult to find homes for only two Colombians for a period of nine months. The host families felt that there should be a month's trial period in which either the host or guest could decide to terminate the arrangement.

7

The Guest's General Role in the Family

It is quite obvious from the talks with the students and Peace Corps trainees that to be "a member of the family" is a very good thing in the minds of the American guests. Yet when we begin to see the meaning of "member of the family" in terms of specific behaviors and motivations, we find considerable ambivalence both in the North American guest and in the Colombian host as to whether they want the American to be "a member of the family." The high value placed upon this phrase by both guest and host seems to be based upon a mutual desire of each to be sociably acceptable to the other and to be viewed as accepting by the other.

The Americans' Ambivalence [1]

The Americans' ambivalence seemed to be a conflict between a desire for emancipation from the older generation (or a desire for independence) and the desire for some special support, help and advice needed while in the foreign environment. In short, there was a strong tendency for the American guest to accept such restrictions, advice, or supervision only when it gave him the support he felt he needed. When he did not feel the need, he tended to reject the aspects of his role in the family that were restrictive, made demands, or involved obligations. He was more interested in the aspects that entitled him to considerations, services, rights, and privileges.

This was not only because he was basically human but also because the mechanisms of social control that generally operate within our own society to get us to accept obligations as well as rights do not operate immediately upon the sojourner in the host culture. The degree to which a person accepts both the obligations and the rights connected with his role is an index of his integration into a particular group of culture.

Seventy-six percent of the students said they felt like members of the Colombian family, yet 35 percent of that group said that it was quite difficult for them to exchange ideas with their family. Of course, this in itself is not a clear contradiction since some of them may find it difficult to exchange ideas with their own families in the United States. However, it is highly doubtful that they could feel like real members of the family when only 12 percent said that they did take the initiative in discussions with the family. Even though 77 percent said that the family did respond when they took the initiative, still 60 percent preferred to spend most of their free time with Americans. This particular group of 49 American students lived with Colombian families, took courses from Colombians in Spanish, and might have felt a need to reduce the pressure of the constant speaking of Spanish by seeking out their American friends in their free time. Of course, this is not totally consistent with wanting to be a member of the Colombian family.

The height of this ambivalence between wanting to be independent and needing some help, is shown when we compare the fact that 70 percent said they preferred to meet people on their own initiative and 35 percent said they felt that the host family should open more social doors for them. Forty-seven percent said they think that CEUCA, the sponsoring American organization, should open more social doors for them. Thus, there is evidence that they were not completely satisfied with the amount of social interaction they have been able to have with Colombians, and yet they did like to feel that they were capable of independently making the social contacts they wanted.

One of the most important locks on the social doors the American guest would like to open he often places there himself. This is the general image of social unacceptability projected by some of the Americans: The guests "acted like they felt superior to Colombians"; they were "generally thoughtless of others"; they did not "dress appropriately for the occasion"; they gave the impression that "they did not care about their reputation among the Colombians"; they "did not bathe frequently"; some of them "smelled bad at times"; and "they do not greet people properly."

Most of the negative images projected by the American guests were products of their own behavior patterns in a context of ignorance of the foreign cultural patterns, yet the interviews with the Americans showed that only rarely did a guest say there was any connection between his own behavior and the closed social doors. Those who thought that the sponsoring American organization should do more to help them socially usually thought that they merely needed help in making the initial contact with a certain kind of Colombian. The doubtful assumption seemed to be that they would know how to take advantage of the opportunity.

Whatever may be the forces of mutual attraction, it seems that there are also forces of mutual repulsion that derive their strength from the simple basic fact that tension and anxiety generated in cross-cultural interaction can be reduced by simply separating the actors, temporarily stopping the interaction. If this is true, the American guest's ambivalence about accepting the role of full-fledged family member is understandable, and the general direction of the solution is to learn how to interact with members of the foreign culture without producing anxiety and tension.

Basically, the American guest's ambivalence is generated by the conflict between his desire to be *independent* of the older generation, especially of his own parents; yet he is more *dependent* because he is in a foreign culture.

Other types of ambivalences develop when the American discovers that the price of being "a member of the family" is more than he would like to pay as he begins gradually to perceive the *obligations* of a family member of his own age. The *gringas*, particularly, may feel that the restrictions and supervision to which they are subjected as a member of the family make them long for dormitory life again.

The Colombian hosts also have ambivalences regarding the American guest's role in the household.

The Colombians' Ambivalence

The Colombian hosts, like the guests, also tended to be ambivalent about the proper role of the American living in their home. We have already seen that they think that a principal motivation for taking *norteamericano* guests is "to earn extra money," yet 87 percent of the señoras said that the American should be treated "like a member of the family" and none said they should be treated "like a guest who pays." Logically, since paying is important and since treating them "like a member of the family" also seems to be important, we would expect a fairly large portion of the señoras to have chosen the fourth response, "like a mixture of these." Yet only 9 percent chose this response in spite of the fact that the Americans were usually treated like some combination of a family member, special guest, and boarder.

This apparent contradiction is resolved to some extent when we analyze the spontaneous remarks of the señoras explaining why they preferred to treat the Americans as members of the family. First, it was clear that most of the señoras prided themselves in being good hostesses who can make anyone in the home feel comfortable. Seventy-four percent of the señoras volunteered the idea that the American should be treated like a member of the family so that he would feel more comfortable. Another 14 percent volunteered that it would also make the family more comfortable. The remaining 11 percent said that if they treated the American like a member of the family, he would in turn treat their own children in the same way.

Being a "member of the family" not only means that the person should be comfortable (in the Colombian way of course), but also that he should assume certain responsibilities of a family member of the same age and sex. The señoras felt that the American should make his own bed neatly, keep his room orderly, leave the bathroom tidy, hang his towel out in the sun to dry, come to meals (lunch and dinner) on time, etc. There are additional responsibilities such as giving gifts on certain occasions, greeting and introducing people, paying one's way, and helping with household chores on special occasions.

Just as some of the American guests hope to carve out a role for themselves which has all of the advantages and none of the disadvantages of the role of family member, some of the señoras also would like to have all of the advantages of a family member who can "take the place of the son or daughter" but who has other advantages one's own son or daughter would not provide.

A large majority of the señoras preferred a North American to a Colombian guest if both paid the same amount. This may seem strange since a Colombian could actually play the role of "member of the family" much more accurately than could the North American. Their reasons included the cross-cultural contact benefits (e.g., learning English) and that the North American would be less bother to the señora than a Colombian.

It was not easy for some of the señoras to articulate *why* or *how* the North American would be less bother. "More trustworthy" included a variety of statements such as "more honest," "dependable in paying what he owes," or "more sincere." "Easier to handle" meant that they thought the American guest was more docile because he felt insecure in the foreign setting and would need help and advice. "More respectful" meant both that North Americans were not so rebellious toward the older generation in general, but more often it meant that the North American male would be more respectful toward the señora, and the female would be more respectful toward the señor than would be a Colombian university student. "Less demanding" in some cases meant that the Colombian guest paying the same amount would demand more special services than an American. "More independent" often meant that the North American was more capable of getting around on his own initiative and would not be so dependent upon the family for his social life. This is in contrast to "too independent" which referred to a person who was not attached to the family and who did not have a warm relationship with the señora. "Males less fresh" usually meant that they viewed the Colombian male as more amorously aggressive which might constitute a problem for the señora.

Many of the señoras felt that the *gringas* needed less supervision than would a Colombian girl of the same age, which is consistent with the idea of "less bother." To measure the extent of this belief among the host señoras we later asked whether they felt that the *colombiana* or the *gringa* guest would require the most supervision. Forty-one percent felt that the *gringa* should be supervised less strictly than the Colombian daughter; 4 percent felt they should have *more* strict supervision; 55 percent felt that the *gringa* should have the same amount of supervision.

Miscommunication About the Guests' Role in the Household

The American guest did not know precisely how to play the role of either "guest" or "member of the family." He did not know how a member of a Colombian family would be treated. Some felt that they were being treated like a special guest rather than a member of the family *because* orange juice and coffee were brought to their bedroom at breakfast time. In several of the homes this is a practice, particularly for the señora or daughters in the home. Other Americans felt that since the Colombians were polite in their greetings and forms of address, they were not treating the American like a member of the family when in fact they were.

The American guests' underestimate of the number of señoras who *think* the American should be treated as a guest could be a reflection of

101

the señora's own ambivalence or of a discrepancy between her idea of how they *should* be treated and how she actually treated them.

> They treat me sort of like a family member but more like a guest because they always make sure I get the best food and often do special favors that the other kids wouldn't get.
>
> They expected me to help around the house like a member of the family, yet if I broke something they made me pay. Also, if you stay a few days longer into the vacation period they make you pay extra.

Miscalculation also results when the American guest tries to discover whether he is being treated like a member of the family with respect to a certain issue by observing how a Colombian family member is treated. In doing this he may fail to compare himself with a Colombian of the same age and sex. For example, "I am reprimanded if my room is disorderly although I clean it myself, change the bed and make the bed, while the kids in the house leave such things to the maid and are a hundred times more disorderly than I."

This sounds like evidence of discrimination but in interviewing this host family it was discovered that "the kids" with whom the American college student was comparing himself were boys seven and nine years old.

In families where there are no members of the guest's age and sex, the guest cannot discover what is appropriate for himself by observing the others. The female guest cannot always assume that if the señora does a certain thing or has certain privileges or duties, the *gringa* should behave in the same way. Nor can the *gringo's* observations of the señor's behavior be a reliable guide, because parents and children occupy a different role and status in any household.

Even though a large minority of the señoras felt that the *gringa* should be less strictly supervised than a *colombiana*, a much larger portion (91 percent) of the American guests felt that the señora expected to exercise less supervision over the *gringa*. Usually the *gringa* was not aware that the señora was quite distraught because of the difficulty in exercising what she felt was adequate supervision. The American girl who tended to take her freedom and independence for granted often felt that she was bending over backward to meet the demands of the culture, but the señora was mainly aware of the shortcomings, particularly those that might damage her reputation.

We also saw a gap in communication in that only 7 percent of the señoras said that they had no preference for a Colombian versus an American guest if the amount paid were equal, but 36 percent of the guests thought their señora felt this way. There was an assumption among many of the Americans that the host families were being paid much more for board and room than could have been collected from a Colombian. In some cases this was because the student did not know how much the señora was paid but *assumed*, since he had paid into the Program the same board and room fee he would have paid on his home campus, this total amount was paid to the host family. He did not realize that a large portion of the cost of board and room in the foreign country went into locating and selecting the host families and in dealing with the developing problems of adjustment between host and guest.

Another possible reason for the American guests' reluctance to think that the señora would actually prefer an American if the pay were equal is that they found it more difficult than did the señoras to see reasons other than money for the señora's taking an American guest. For example, when the guests were asked why their señora might prefer an American, none of them had the idea that the señora would feel that the American would be less bother than a Colombian guest. All of the reasons they could give were in the cross-cultural experience category.

Another area of miscommunication was revealed in the fact that many guests did not realize the extent to which the host families would support their role as student. Some guests felt that there was a conflict between their role as student versus family member. The Americans reported in the interviews that their host family wanted them to skip classes for a day or two in order to take a long weekend trip with them, and they worried that the family would be insulted if they did not go. We asked the señoras, "If you were planning a trip over a long weekend and you invited your American guest to go with you, should he be willing to miss classes for two days if he really wanted to go?" Then the guests were asked to indicate how they thought their señoras would answer the question.

The guests greatly underestimated the proportion (79.5 percent versus 4.5 percent) of the señoras who felt the guests should not miss classes to go on a trip. A few of the señoras volunteered the comment that they should come on the trip because they should not stay in the house without the family there, particularly if the guest were a *gringa*. We cannot explain why more Americans did not realize how the señoras felt about interfering with their studies, nor do we know that their saying that the "studies come first" was not simply a polite excuse to leave the foreign guest behind. To take him might have caused overcrowding if they were driving, or the American might not have intended to pay his way to the extent expected by the host, or the Colombian family may have wanted some time away from the foreign guest they see every day. The student may also have been hopefully rationalizing his own desires to escape from his studies by saying that the family would be insulted if he put his studies above a long weekend trip with them.

Formal Customs of Courtesy

The North American can easily give a Colombian the impression that he does not want to meet people or participate in social events because he does not observe the social rituals that are so important in Latin America. Even after the guests begin to sense the vital importance of these "superficial customs," he still may not know how to do them correctly.

The host-family señoras feel that they can separate the sheep from the goats among American guests by whether they make the proper polite responses such as greeting, introducing, and thanking people. None of the señoras interviewed took a neutral position on whether their particular American guest was polite in this respect. The señoras felt that the Americans' weakest point was in knowing how to greet people. To some hosts this meant that the guest did not know how or when to shake hands.

Shaking hands

To the Colombians the Americans seemed to have some reluctance to shake hands.

> His customs were typically North American. Even in the way he greeted you. You know the Americans don't like this thing about shaking your hand.

> As an advisor to the North Americans as foreign students here in Colombia, I tell them that the only time they don't shake hands on greeting someone is when both hands are broken. It is difficult to impress them with the importance of this simple act.

Although there is a difference in the amount of handshaking that is customary in different regions of the United States,[2] in general the *bogotanos* tended to shake hands much more than the North Americans were accustomed to. The American at first had to force himself to shake hands with even 10 people when he arrived and left a dinner party, for example. The American college student's tendency to minimize the greeting rituals is even more emphasized when he is abroad where he feels unsure about the language and the accompanying actions. At first it takes considerable effort on the American's part even when he understands what the *bogotanos* expect. In time it becomes a habit and, when he returns to the United States, he catches himself extending his hand in many situations when it is not expected.

Here are some of the ways in which handshaking is different from the practice in most parts of the United States.

Shake hands more frequently. The probability that two North Americans will shake hands upon meeting depends upon (among other things) how recently they have seen each other. It is clear that the time lapse that requires the "reshaking" of hands is much shorter in Colombia than in the United States. For example, on entering the home of a friend or acquaintance it is expected that you shake hands even though you may have seen the person only a few minutes before.

Shake hands with more people. On entering a place where a social or business gathering is taking place you shake hands with each person, up to as many as 20 persons. In very large groups of 50 or more, it is customary to stop at each small group and shake hands with each person present.

Shake hands on more occasions. The North American is less inclined to shake hands when he leaves a group than when he arrives. Colombians shake hands as frequently upon leaving as when arriving.

Men do not wait for women to take initiative. When a man greets a woman, he does not wait for the woman to offer her hand because it is customary for women to shake hands on all of the same occasions as would a man.

The woman-to-woman handshake is different. It is a custom for women to shake hands with women, particularly after the first time they have met, in a style different from the man-to-man or woman-to-man handshake. They frequently shake hands by simultaneously grasping each other's right forearm. If the North American girl first experiences this without any prior warning, she may be surprised.

> I went to this party at a relative's house where there were several Colombians I had met once before. The hostess shook hands with me like this [grasping forearm], and I thought maybe she was blind and had missed my hand or something.

> The first time I went to a party I was lucky because I had a chance to observe my señora welcoming guests to our home and noticed that she shook hands with the men one way and with the women another. Of course I didn't know how general this was, but then when I went to another house party I was on the lookout for it.

> For the first month or so I didn't realize that I wasn't shaking hands right, but I noticed a bit of fumbling confusion sometimes as our hands met. Then later I discovered that this was because I grabbed their hand before they could get past mine to clasp my arm like they do. I just never thought that they would shake hands with a man one way and with a woman another.

The man-to-man handshake is less vigorous. The American men also had a problem with the manner of shaking hands even though it is essentially the same act as in the United States. Many of the Americans were accustomed to a vigorous grasp and felt that many of the *bogotanos* had an insipid handshake: "You'd think some of these men are sick from the way they shake hands. It is like holding a dead fish. It's hard to believe that they mean it. They are certainly not very enthusiastic."

Similarly, some of the *bogotanos* interpreted the American's vigorous handshake as another expression of his feeling of superiority: "The Americans say that we are so concerned with *machismo*, in trying to prove our masculinity, but when they shake your hand they seem to be engaging in some kind of contest to prove that they are stronger."

In the eyes of some *bogotanos* both the American's reluctance to shake hands and his "aggressive" manner when he does so can contribute to that image, shared by many host families, that the American thinks he is superior to the *bogotano*. At the same time, the American can get the impression that the *bogotano* is not warmly enthusiastic about meeting him.

These differences in handshaking customs may not exhaust the whole range of differences,[3] but they include the most common cross-cultural dissonances encountered by the Americans and Colombians.

Thanking Colombians

A majority of the señoras thought that the North American guests knew "how to thank a person for a favor." Significantly, none took a neutral position on this issue. Again this shows the tendency for the host to put his guest clearly in either the positive or negative category with respect to his manners. We must, however, make a distinction between knowing how and actually doing it. If a Colombian thought his guest did know how but did not thank him properly for a favor, he concluded that the American did not appreciate the favors done for him. This interpretation is consistent with that fact that despite the majority who agreed that the American knows how, only half agreed that "they appreciate the favors they receive."

In the depth interviews with the señoras we found a few hints as to what was lacking in the American's attempt to thank them.

> . . . and we took her on a picnic at Zipaquirá, went to the Salt Cathedral, took her to the market to take pictures, and then went to show her Villa de Leiva which is a long trip so we stayed overnight in Villa. When we got back home, all she said was "gracias"!

> He was interested in seeing some of the sights in Bogotá, so we went to Monserrate on the cable car, went through the museum of the Quinta de Bolívar, to the Cathedral, the Plaza de Bolívar, and the Plaza de la Constitución and even

to the market which we never would go to, but he wanted to see it. We went to lunch at the Casa Vieja and returned home at about seven. When we got home, he just said "gracias" and that he was tired so he went up to his room.

The key to the problem is expressed concisely in the phrase "all he said was 'gracias.'" This is enough if someone has just lent a person a match, but not adequate in cases of larger favors. The following excerpts from the señoras' interviews give a strong stamp of approval to the guest who shows his appreciation more profusely.

> ... he wasn't a typical American in this way. He had very good manners. He was well brought up. For example, we invited him to the soccer game, then went swimming at the Club Militar and then to dinner at La Chesa. He was very appreciative. He said, *"Qué buena la excursión! Fue sumamente interesante para mí. Fue muy amable de su parte el haberme invitado. Es el día más especial que he tenido aquí en Bogotá. Muchísimas gracias por todo."*
>
> He seemed to always appreciate little things we did for him. He was so different from the first student who would just say "gracias" in a very dry way.

It is not strange that the host does not teach the guest how to show his appreciation, because the role of host would preclude appearing to demand profuse thanks. If the guest does not do some equivalent favor for the host, he cannot learn by observing the example of the host's reaction to a favor. The breakdown in communication is facilitated by the señora's assumption that the guest knows how to express appreciation but does not feel any appreciation in a particular instance.

Greetings

The *bogotano's* feeling that the North Americans did not "greet people properly" was also related to the Americans' failure to say either "hello" or "goodbye." It was not necessary to ask the señoras specifically whether the American guest greeted people properly. It was clear that this was such an essential factor in their judgment of the American that in the depth interviews they would mention the greeting problem when they were asked questions such as: "What kind of a person was your last guest?" The responses most frequently given could be categorized into different dimensions of etiquette such as greeting people properly, thanking people, giving of gifts, and paying one's way.

> Well, in general the American girls never say hello. I think it is only natural to greet people when you come into the house but they never do.
>
> They never came to say hello and sometimes we were here. That bothered us.
>
> Some of the Americans that came were very badly brought up in that they would not greet you.
>
> Sometimes we would have parties and introduce them to my friends too. But later

when you meet them again they do not even say hello to you. Maybe they don't remember us.

This last statement may involve much more than the simple reluctance to greet people. It may be due to a situation that typically confronts any foreigner who is new in the community. When he goes to any group function, he may be the only stranger to the group, while all of the members are strangers to him. They have only one new face to remember while the foreigner has many. Nevertheless, there is considerable evidence that the American did tend to greet people less frequently and to be less formal or profuse when he did greet them.

The fact that the *bogotanos* appreciated those guests who did not "behave like typical Americans" can be seen in the following positive statements coming from the host señoras:

> He was very polite and nice. He used to say hello and when he left the house he would say goodbye.
>
> Ricardo would usually say hello and goodbye but some days he forgot it. That was very different from Russ who would even look for me to say goodbye. It was a big difference.
>
> Whenever she would come in and there were people here, she would greet everyone and stay a little while before she went upstairs. She said goodbye in a very friendly way. All my friends liked her very much.
>
> When there were people here she would come and would say hello as if she were a member of the family.

The majority of the señoras preferred that the American guest seek them out to greet them even in the routine daily return to the home. The proportion who preferred to be sought out rises when the American returns after sightseeing on Saturday afternoon, and all the señoras felt the guest should greet them upon returning from a two-day absence. The señoras, as *dueñas* of the home, not only considered it polite, but also liked to know when the American was in the house just as they would like to know when one of their own children or their husband returned.

The use of adiós

The word *adiós* as a greeting was a source of mutual puzzlement between Colombians and North Americans. For example, the American was puzzled when he met a Colombian acquaintance on the street who simply said, "Adiós," and continued walking. The American in this case tended to think of *adiós* as being part of the leave-taking ritual, and therefore, not to be used between two people as they approach each other on the street. In English the American would say, "Hello," "Hi," or "Good morning," and *adiós* seems to be inappropriate. Actually, the Colombian uses *adiós* in those situations where two people are going to pass each other without stopping, or if they do not wish to be detained. In effect it combined the idea of *hello* and *goodbye* in one word.

The Colombians, in turn, were puzzled by the North American's use of *adiós* as a parting formality. The American seemed to think of it as meaning simply *goodbye*, therefore after he had spent the evening with a group he would say only, "Adiós," and leave. This was not enough. It was considered cold unless some phrase were added such as, *mucho gusto de verte, que estés muy bien,* or *saludos en tu casa.* The incorrect interpretation of the use of *adiós* in these two situations was a source of mutual irritation.

Greeting versus leavetaking

The North American guests were sometimes confused by the use of *"Buenos días!" "Buenas tardes!"* and *"Buenas noches!"* to mean both hello and goodbye depending on the situation. A majority of the Americans seemed to think of these phrases as equivalent to "Good morning!" "Good afternoon!" and "Good evening!"[4] and therefore equal to a form of hello but not goodbye.

> When she said, *"buenos días"* I thought she had just arrived or that she thought I had just arrived. I felt that I had been talking to her in the group of Colombian students just before we went into the classroom, but when she said *"buenos días"* I was a bit confused because I thought I must be wrong in thinking she was the one I had just talked to. Later I realized that this was because I interpreted the *buenos días* to mean good morning in the sense of hello not goodbye.
>
> It took a while before I was sure that *buenos días* alone would not tell you whether they were saying hello or goodbye. It depends upon what else they say, if anything.

Inquiring about the family

When greeting a married person who is not accompanied by the family, it is always polite to ask about the spouse and children. This is automatic with the *bogotanos* but takes practice for the North American.

Using titles

In greetings, as in any form of direct address, it is customary to use the person's title. Never should we say, *"Buenos días, Martínez,"* or *"Buenas tardes, José."* It is much more polite to say *"Buenos días, señor Martínez,"* or *"Buenas tardes, don José."* The feminine equivalents of *señora* and *doña* are used in the same way. A specific degree such as *licenciado* can be used also.

In cases where someone has a professional status, the last name is often preceded by *doctor*. A student addressing a professor should always use the title *profesor* or *doctor* before the last name. *Doctor* is used much more generally than in the United States to refer to anyone with education or higher status. In Bogotá anyone with a college education may be addressed as *doctor*. To avoid confusion we must refer to a physician as *el médico* not *el doctor*. The lower class and the *campesinos* often address anyone in a higher socioeconomic class as *doctor*, which often surprises the American undergraduate student.

Of course, when using titles in indirect address the definite article is added, as in *la señora, el doctor*, but there is a very important exception to this rule in the case of *doña*. We should never refer to a woman as *la doña* which would mean "the madam" of a house of prostitution to some Colombians. This would severely shock a *bogotano* even though he knew it was not intentional on the part of the American. In some contexts it could appear to be quite intentional and would damage the American's image by lending credence to the idea, "Americans don't care about their reputation among Colombians."

The North American is often at a loss in addressing a nun or priest in Spanish. In general the priest should be *Padre* in direct address and *el padre* in indirect address parallel to the English *Reverend* and *the Reverend*. On some occasions the form *su reverencia* is also used. In addressing a nun the form *madre* or *hermana* is used depending on the nun's order and her position in the hierarchy. It is always safest to call her *madre* since this is the higher status. When possible the American should be alert to follow the lead of the Colombians in the particular situation. The Bishop is addressed as *su excelencia*.

Some of the Americans who were from Protestant or Jewish background found it very difficult and unnatural to use these forms of address which in their minds was like calling a stranger father, mother or sister. Others felt that it implied some theological commitment on their part to Catholicism. Those who thought of it as simply a title to designate one's function in society did not find these titles difficult to use.

Introductions

It is a common practice for someone who is about to make an introduction to ask, "*¿Ustedes no se conocen?*" Then if one or both say, "*No tengo el gusto*," one of three things might happen. The two may shake hands and give their names simultaneously. The person making the introduction may add, "*Quisiera presentar a mi amigo*," or "*a mi primo*," or "*a mi esposa*," without giving the name, and the pair shake hands and give their own names simultaneously. The person making the introduction may give both names and they will shake hands. The first two forms are very common, but they make it very difficult for the American to hear the other person's name which is being given just as he gives his own name to the Colombian. Yet the system is often advantageous in that the introducer may not remember a person's name at the moment, so he can simply say, *"Quisiera presentar a mi estudiante,"* and then it is up to the two persons to give their own names which allows the introducer to learn the person's full name. If the introducer uses the third form, he must not only be sure he has the correct name but must also remember to use the title with the article to indicate indirect address, *"Quisiera presentar al doctor García."*

Even though many of the American guests understood the correct forms of introductions, they were still considered aloof in situations that called for introducing themselves. For example, a guest would arrive home at 5:00 p.m. and find some strangers at the house in the living room. Since the señora was not with them at the moment, he might pass by them with a simple "Buenas tardes," as he headed for the stairway without stopping to introduce himself or giving the visitors a chance to introduce themselves. The *bogotano* hosts felt that the American guests failed to introduce themselves at times when it was considered appropriate. This was not due to the guest's general reluctance to introduce people because a majority of the hosts felt the guest did very well in introducing his friends to the family.

Another aspect of the introduction situation that bothered some Colombians and gave the impression of the American's being aloof was what we might call the "hit-and-run" tendency. Instead of seeing the introduction as a prologue to a pleasant friendly chat, the American would immediately try to leave.

> . . . for example, you would introduce him to your friends and he would say "hello" very kindly, but then he would immediately try to leave the situation.

> She came home that afternoon and I introduced her to some people in the living room and instead of sitting down and talking a moment, she just said, *"Con su permiso,"* and went upstairs to her room.

The lack of this knowledge could result in the American giving the impression that he is "aloof and superior" if he did not stay or that he was a "pushy intruder" if he did.

Using *tú* versus *usted*

The English speaker often has difficulty in deciding between the use of the formal *usted* and the familiar *tú* forms of pronouns. Historically, he has lost his choice between *you* and *thou* and feels an added burden in making this decision when speaking Spanish. He has the linguistic problem of knowing both forms of pronouns and verb conjugations plus the more complex nonlinguistic problem of sensing when to use each.

He often arrives in Latin America with the idea that there is one simple consistent pattern for the use of these two forms. To the contrary, it is highly probable that this usage pattern varies from one region to another, from one social class to another, and according to other more subtle difference in the social situations in which the conversations take place.

The Americans were confused about the proper use of the familiar form. Some had obtained contradictory ideas from different Colombians they had asked for advice.

In general, *tú* was used when the señora addressed her husband, her children, and when her children addressed her. Most señoras used *usted* to address their maids. However, there is enough lack of unanimity to confuse the Americans. The señoras who chose the "other" category were almost all of two types—those who said they used both *tú* and *usted* depending on the occasion and those who used *su merced* instead of *tú*.

There is a possibility that the form used with children would depend upon their age. It was suggested by one respondent that with smaller children they used *usted* and for older ones *tú*. The exceptions to the general pattern are enough to shake the security of the American trying to learn the pattern.

The fact that most of the señoras used *tú* in addressing their children, and most of the children addressed their mothers in this way, would lead us to predict that these same señoras would expect their American guests to address them with *tú* since a large majority of them also expect the American to act "like a member of the family." To test this idea which is very relevant to the American's role in the family, we asked the señoras about the conditions under which *tú* should be used between the guest and the host. We distinguished between the different sex combinations of host and guest and tried to determine how soon the *tú* relationship could be established. Then to determine the amount of guest-host communication on this point, we asked the American guests how they thought their particular señora would answer the questions.

In all four relationships the guests erred in the direction of assuming that they should never use *tú*. More of the Americans than the Colombians thought it was necessary to wait until after a certain relationship was established. Fewer Americans than Colombians felt that *tú* should be used from the beginning. The proportion of hosts choosing each category correlates mainly with whether the relationship is between persons of the same sex or opposite sexes. More say not to use *tú* when it is between opposite sexes.

When we ask whether the American guests were correct in perceiving the hosts' preference for *tú*, one clear pattern emerged. The American guests consistently underestimated the hosts' preference for using *tú* with their American guests. Fewer Americans expected *tú* to be used from the beginning, and more of them thought it should never be used than did the Colombians. This could be another factor supporting the Colombians' image of the "superior American" who does not want to be "a member of the family."

In some cases this unfortunate image was avoided when the señora took the initiative in directly instructing the guest.

> Three days after I was here I was told to address everybody as *tú* because we were a family.
>
> The señora said to me "You are a member of the family and you are not going to address us with *usted*!!"
>
> My family told me that I was a member of the family and was to address them as *tú*.

The lack of unanimity regarding the appropriate use of *tú* was also graphically demonstrated by the fact that of the four Colombian interviewers who interviewed most of the *señoras*, one always used the familiar form in the interview. When I asked her why she did this, she said, "in order to get their confidence." Other interviewers with the same educational background and socioeconomic status used the formal *usted* in all interviews.

In view of these inconsistencies, it is highly probable that there are not only regional and social class differences in the use of the familiar form, but also there may be a historical trend toward the use of only one of the forms or a breaking down of the rigid distinction between their use. In any event the simple one-sentence explanations of the use of the familiar form, still found in Spanish textbooks for English speakers, seems too simple to accurately reflect the realities in Bogotá.

Three salient results emerged from this exploratory study which are relevant to the central problem of communication barriers: There was no unanimity among these señoras regarding the appropriate use of the familiar form; the American guests often did not know when they were expected to use the familiar form and so failed to use it in situations where it was expected by the hosts; this failure was often interpreted by the Colombians as a symptom of the American's desire to remain aloof from the family.

If the Colombian did not directly suggest using *tú*, the American was often at a loss to know what to do. In some cases they were aware that the hosts had started using *tú* in addressing them, but they did not know whether this was a dependable sign that they should also begin to use *tú*. When one American tried to advise another on the problem, confusion often would result.

> My Colombian sister told me that in Bogotá *usted* is used more with close friends and *tú* with acquaintances and strangers.
>
> In my (Colombian) family, I would feel uncomfortable using *tú* with either the señor or the señora unless they asked me to. The girl should with the señor only if she completely trusts him and doesn't feel that it would embarrass the señora. They are starting to use *tú* much more with me but I won't with them until they ask me.
>
> Here in Bogotá, it seems to me that you only use *tú* with your boyfriend. Even within the family they use *usted* with each other.
>
> In Colombia *tú* is used less frequently than in Mexico. For example, even my (Colombian) twin brothers use the *usted* form. So I think it is better to treat it as a grammatical thing than as a personal reflection.

It is clear that a more thorough study should be made of the use of *tú* to determine the causes of this variation and search for dependable tactics for the American to use in specific situations to select the appropriate form of address.

Gift-giving Patterns

Most of the señoras felt that the American guests did bring gifts "on occasions when they should." It is highly probable that the Colombians were not so much paying a compliment to the American's knowledge of what was appropriate to give on certain occasions as they were expressing faith in the American's generous intent. This interpretation is consistent with the fact that the American often did not know that he was supposed to bring a present in one situation, while he gave a present in another situation where it was not customary to do so. The Colombian's and the American's views of the relative importance of giving a gift on 24 different occasions are compared in Table 2. The 24 situations are arranged in rank order according to the amount and direction of the cross-cultural discrepancy. In Situation 1 the Americans would be perceived as the "most negligent," and in Situation 24 they would be perceived as "overgenerous" by the Colombians.

Sometimes the American who did not bring a gift to a first communion party, for example, would feel embarrassed when he saw that others had

Table 2

Occasions for Giving Gifts: Colombian Hosts' and the American Guests' Feeling of the Importance of the Guests Giving a Gift on Certain Occasions

SITUATION	INDEX OF IMPORTANCE* SEÑORA	GUEST†	DIFFERENCE
1. Notified of but not invited to host-family member's first communion‡	124	47	77
2. Notified of but not invited to host-family member's baptism	86	38	48
3. Host-family member ordained into the priesthood	136	100	36
4. Her *novio* has a birthday but no party	186	153	33
5. His *novia* has a birthday but no party	198	173	25
6. Invited to a special party by the host family	102	81	21
7. Invited to a first communion breakfast	139	122	17
8. Invited to a graduation ceremony	165	150	15
9. Invited to a baptism ceremony	122	110	12
10. Señora just had a baby in the hospital	155	147	8
11. Invited to a first communion ceremony	153	148	5
12. Host-family member graduates but no party	140	140	0
13. Twenty-fifth wedding anniversary party	150	159	− 9
14. Fifth wedding anniversary party	111	127	−16
15. Baptism party	133	150	−17
16. Dinner at another family's home	27	46	−19
17. Invited to a wedding	157	177	−20
18. Host-family member sick in the hospital	89	109	−20
19. Guest returns to host family after a weekend	41	70	−29
20. To host family at Christmas time	159	192	−33
21. To host family when guest returns from vacation in United States	140	179	−39
22. Guest receives wedding announcement	27	67	−40
23. Guest leaving for the U.S. at end of stay	96	136	−40
24. Guest invited to confirmation ceremony	46	117	−71

* The "importance index" was derived by giving the value of 2 to a response of "it's important" and a value of 1 to "it's all right but not important" and a value of 0 to "generally no gift is given."
† This is based on the American guest's estimate of how the señora would answer the same question.
‡ When the guest is informed of the event but not invited to the ceremony.

brought presents. Actually, such embarrassment was sometimes needless because the invitation was issued to the family as a unit; when the señora told the American that he was invited, he mistakenly assumed that she was merely relaying an invitation which had been aimed at him as a separate entity. Often on occasions such as weddings, confirmations, baptisms, or graduations, the family is invited as a unit; therefore the American might be automatically included as a "member of the family" depending on his relationship with them.

Many of the Americans did quite well by simply asking the señora, *"¿Cuál es la costumbre en cuanto a. . .?"* However, this can cause considerable confusion because the American does not understand the cultural context of the occasion well enough to ask all of the vital questions. This confusion is shown in the following excerpt from an interview with a Peace Corps trainee.

> I know that I had been invited by Fernando, one of the students at *Universidad Nacional*, to go to his younger sister Raquel's high school graduation party. I had a whole week's warning so I asked my señora if it was customary for me to give a present to the sister. We even discussed what sort of thing might be good to give. So I went shopping and bought a bottle of perfume on the señora's advice. But was I ever embarrassed! When I got to the party with the present in my hot little hand, I found that no one else had brought a present. It was a very special occasion too because of the way people dressed and there were lots of flowers all over the house. I did not want to appear to be a *gringo* "showoff" so I didn't give the present. At first I thought I'd just play it cool since I arrived fairly early. I watched to see what the Colombian guys brought—which was nothing! So I just left the present in the pocket of my top coat. I still have it all wrapped up ready to give on some other occasion.

Actually all of the people who came to the party had given Raquel a present in honor of the occasion. What the American did not know was that Raquel went to a girl's school, and there had been a small party at school where her girl friends had brought presents. Also, the boys who came to this party had sent flowers to the home in advance so they arrived at the door empty handed as observed by the American. Fernando and the other members of the family had given Raquel a present privately.

This incident illustrates a basic problem in cross-cultural communication. Even though there is no language barrier and the native is perfectly willing to answer any question about the problem, the foreigner fails to ask the appropriate questions. The pattern of questions asked and omitted is in itself a manifestation of the cultural background of the asker. Certain questions are not asked because we unconsciously assume that we know the "only possible" answer.

In this very exploratory investigation of the subject of gift giving in Bogotá, we became aware of some of the variables that determine whether or not a gift is to be given: the occasion, the channel through which the invitation came, whether the invitation was issued to an individual or a family, and the social status relationship between the persons involved. It is not enough to know whether a gift is appropriate, but it is also necessary to know when it is given, where it is given, how it is given, how it is wrapped, to whom it is given, and what is said when the gift is presented. Of course, it is important to know what kinds of presents are appropriate for various types of occasions. The sex combination of giver and receiver has some bearing upon the type of present considered appropriate.

We obtained information from the señoras on the type of gift appropriate on that occasion where the Americans most frequently and appropriately brought gifts—the birthday party. To determine the importance of the sex combination, the señora was asked about the four combinations as shown in Table 3. Certain patterns particularly interesting to Americans are visible:

1. No alcoholic beverages or smoking accessories are suggested as gifts to girls.

2. Flowers are suggested to be given to girls by *both* girls and boys but not to be given to boys.

3. Boy-to-girl flowers are suggested three times as often as girl-to-girl flowers.

4. Books are suggested as presents to boys six times as often as to girls.

5. Pen and pencil sets are suggested for gifts to boys only.

6. Compacts are given only by girls.

7. Porcelain figurines were suggested as girl-to-girl presents four times as often as for boy-to-girl presents.

8. Dolls were suggested as boy-to-girl presents. (It is not uncommon for girls in their late teens and early 20s to receive large stuffed animal dolls from boyfriends. To many North Americans this seemed childish.)

9. Manicure sets were suggested as gifts only to boys. (The *bogotano* middle-class man is much more conscious of the condition of his nails than is the American. The manicurist in the all-male barbershop in Bogotá is heavily patronized. In many shops there are as many manicurists as barber chairs.)

10. Certain gifts were suggested in all but the boy-to-girl relationship. (For example, lotions, soaps, handkerchiefs and things for the desk. To an American lotions seemed as likely a present as perfume which was second in priority in the boy-to-girl list.)

Table 3

Señoras' Suggestions for Birthday Gifts

GIRLS GIVE TO GIRLS	BOYS GIVE TO GIRLS	GIRLS GIVE TO BOYS	BOYS GIVE TO BOYS
Cosmetics	Flowers	Books	Books
Porcelain figurines	Perfumes	After-shave lotion	After-shave lotion
Flowers	Costume jewelry	Phonograph records	Tie clips and cuff links
Lotions	Porcelain figurines	Tie clips and cuff links	Necktie
Perfumes	Phonograph records	Things for the desk	Pen and pencil set
Compact	Books	Pen and pencil set	Phonograph records
Costume jewelry	Dolls	Wallet	Shaving equipment
Handkerchiefs		Necktie	Cigarette lighter
Decorations for bedroom		Handkerchief	Wallet
Phonograph records		Cigarette lighter	Ash tray
Books		Ash tray	Handkerchief
Things for the desk		Manicure set	Manicure set

To discover the extent to which the American guests were aware of these gift-giving patterns, we asked them what they thought "their señora" would suggest under the same conditions. They seemed to be quite aware of some of the points where the Colombian pattern differed from their own. But those they were not aware of were the following:

1. That a college age boy could give a large stuffed animal doll to a Colombian girl.

2. A significant number of Americans mentioned a box of candy which was not mentioned by any of the señoras.

3. Porcelain figurines were never mentioned by the Americans as a gift to girls but were high on the priority list of the Colombians.

4. The Americans mentioned "an expensive night out" as a boy-to-girl gift, but this was never mentioned by the Colombians.

5. The Americans never suggested a manicure set as a gift to a boy.

6. The Americans mentioned books for girls almost as often as for boys, while the Colombians thought of books as a high priority item for boys but a low priority for girls.

The appropriate manner of giving and receiving gifts is very important to the *bogotano* host families. To them a good person is *"una persona detallista,"* not literally a "detailed person" but a person who does considerate things for his acquaintances including giving the right gift at the right time and doing little favors appropriate to the occasion.

Those Americans who happened to learn the appropriate gift-giving pattern were perceived as more *detallista*, as caring more about what Colombians thought of them, as caring more for Colombians, and therefore, more interested in being included in the activities of the family circle. This family circle is sometimes very wide in view of the importance of extended relationships in Colombia, even in a city of two million.

Furthermore, those Americans who learned the pattern had a greater feeling of security and more readily accepted invitations. It can be just as problematic to give gifts when they are not called for as it is to fail to give a gift when it is customary to do so. In the first instance we can unintentionally make people feel obligated or be accused of acting like a "rich American," and in the second instance we can be perceived as simply a "tightwad," an inconsiderate person, or a voluntary social isolate.

Paying One's Way

Another symptom of the American guest's confusion regarding his role in the Colombian host family is his embarrassment over the sharing of certain expenses.

> We went to a birthday party on Saturday night, and there was one girl there that I danced and talked with mainly during the evening. She was with her mother. The party seemed to break up rather suddenly at about 3:00 a.m. I had said goodnight to the hostess and was standing out on the front step wondering how I was going to get home when this girl and her mother came out. The mother said, "Do you have a ride?" and I said, "No, I don't," so she said the only way is to get a taxi on *Carrera Trece*. So, being gallant, I said, "I'll go to *Trece* and catch one and come by here to pick you up." So she thanked me and I was back in about three minutes with a taxi which was very lucky. I could have been an hour just as well. As it turned out their home was beyond mine by about 20 blocks, so when I got to my stop I didn't know what to do exactly so I saw that the meter read 4 pesos, so I gave the mother 5 pesos to pay when they arrived at their house and got out and said, "Buenas noches."

The American actually made two errors. He should have taken the mother and daughter home first and then retraced his route to his own home. It would be considered very important for a gentleman to see the women home under these circumstances. To be considered socially proper he should also have paid the taxi fare. Not because any woman who can

119

get any man to bring a taxi and share it is entitled to have her fare paid, but in this case where both were guests at the same house party, where the man had given attention to one girl during the evening and when he needed a taxi for himself, the Colombian would assume that the man intended to see her home and pay the taxi fare. The American boy who had never seen the girl before the party did not see any connection between devoting a certain amount of attention to the girl at the party and being obligated to pay the fare.

Let us look at another situation in which the American unwittingly became obligated to pay.

> A funny thing happened to me out at the *Universidad Nacional* on Friday. I was eating a snack at the coffee shop in the social science building. I was with two *colombiano* students. One of the girls in the sociology department walked by and I said to her, "Would you like to join us?" and she said, "Muchas gracias," and sat down. We were just having a *tinto* and *bizcochos* when she joined us. She ordered a sandwich, *tinto*, and *bizcochos*, and we all joked around a bit. Then she said she had another class and got up and left without paying. She was very polite and said, "Muchísimas gracias," and "Con su permiso," but did not even try to pay. Then the waiter came over and gave me the check for the whole bag.

The American knew her as a student in his sociology class but did not have any close acquaintance with her. He did not know whether she was just a gold-digger, had simply forgotten to pay the check, or whether this was standard operating procedure in the culture. Actually, he probably had obligated himself to pay, depending upon precise wording the American used in asking her to join them.

The tendency for Americans to go "Dutch treat" with a group of friends (particularly if all are of the same sex) is very strong. This custom is well known to many Colombians who do not call it "Dutch treat" but *"a la americana"* or *"según la costumbre norteamericana."* This is the source of confusion in the following accounts by the American guests.

> When I tried to pay for my ticket at the movie he wouldn't let me. He said that he had invited me and he would pay! The second time I had suggested the movie because it was one I had wanted to see for years. When we got to the ticket window this time I was ahead of him so I could be sure to pay for my own tickets this time. It was just that I didn't want to go on being treated as a special guest forever. But when I paid for my ticket and went ahead to the ticket taker, I was amazed because Mario had not bought a ticket at all. When he started past the ticket taker he wouldn't let Mario in. Then I realized what had happened. I guess he had assumed I had bought two tickets instead of one. It was very embarrassing!

While this American thought he was making progress in getting the "Dutch treat" system accepted in his case, the Colombian thought that the American was going to reciprocate by taking him to the movie.

120

Some of the Colombian hosts were aware of the fact that even the North American women had been brought up under the "Dutch treat" system and thought that the *gringas* might be taking advantage of the fact that they were expected to pay in fewer situations in Bogotá.

> The last guest I had was a *gringa* and she admitted to me that when she went out with Colombians even in a group, she didn't have to spend any money because they always paid for everything. She said that when she went out with Americans she had to spend her own money.

> When the *gringas* come here to Bogotá they are taken by the fact that the Colombian boys are generous . . . that they buy the tickets for them to go to the movies, they buy them chocolates and pay the taxi for them.

> The American boys seem to have more embarrassing situations because they are expected to pay more often than the *gringas*. For example, Jim had a problem when his girlfriend invited him to a club. It was her birthday so she ordered some drinks for them all . . . then later he ordered something for them all. . . . But when the bill came it was all for him, so he told them that part of the bill belonged to the ladies, but they said, "This is not a custom here," so he said, "That's fine, then I will pay for it." Later he told me, "I was so nervous, I always put my foot in it."

The Americans were perceived as less generous in relation to paying their way than in relation to giving gifts on appropriate occasions. Only 32 percent of the señoras would *disagree* with the statement, "Americans don't offer to pay when they should." More were willing to disagree (43 percent) with the idea, "They invite you and don't pay." Nevertheless, the number who did agree suggests that many errors are being made in communication where the Colombian feels that he has been invited as a guest of the American, while the American plans to go "Dutch treat." That there was still less agreement with the statement, "They always show off their money," is encouraging.

Many of the Colombians seemed to feel that their particular guest did not fit the stereotype of the "rich *norteamericano*," but that he was somewhat budget conscious and was trying to cut corners on expenses, or that at least he did not strive to assert his affluence by paying others' expenses in social situations.

This was interpreted in different ways by different Colombians. Some thought it was a pity that these people who were really rich were unwilling to spend any money but would let others spend it on them. Others were very happy that the American restrained his generosity because it would have obligated them to reciprocate in a way that some could not afford. Others thought of the Americans as essentially students who never have money to spend.

It is very interesting to note that in those few cases where the Colombians thought the Americans *did* "show off their money," the

Americans seemed to be completely at a loss to explain how the impression could have been given. I overheard the following conversation between two Americans in the lobby of the CEUCA building. In the quiet of 8:15 on Tuesday morning the following conversation could be overheard by three Colombians—the receptionist in the lobby, a secretary who was talking with her, and the librarian in the room adjoining the lobby. The interviews show the American's lack of awareness of how he gives Colombians the impression that he is rich.

HELEN. Margie, how did you like your weekend in Girardot?

MARGIE. I'm glad you asked, Helen, because it was terrific! We took a trip up the river Magdalena for half a day and had a ball swimming at the Tocarema pool in the afternoon when it was too hot to do anything else. Then we ran around the market and watched rafts of bamboo going downstream. How did you do in Cartagena, you lucky dog?

HELEN. It was great! We flew with just one stop in Medellín and stayed Friday and Saturday night. We did everything there was to do. We stayed at the El Caribe where you have both a pool and the surf, explored the Fuerte de San Felipe, and ate in an ancient fort converted into a restaurant. We arrived there by boat which is more fun than the taxi. It was great but I'm broke because I spent a thousand pesos in addition to airfare and hotel, but I guess it was worth it!

Interview with Alicia, the Colombian receptionist.

INTERVIEWER. Frankly, what are your feelings about the *norteamericanos* you have known here at CEUCA?

ALICIA. Generally, they are *muy amables* and they seem interested in learning about Colombia.

INTERVIEWER. I see, and what sort of background do they seem to come from?

ALICIA. Most of them are Protestants, of course.

INTERVIEWER. Of course, and what about their economic circumstances?

ALICIA. They are typical Americans I guess.

INTERVIEWER. In what way?

ALICIA. They have quite a bit of money.

INTERVIEWER. How can you tell that?

ALICIA. Yesterday, one *gringa* was talking about her trip to Cartagena on the weekend and spent a thousand pesos in addition to airfare and hotel, and she dresses very well all the time. Also I notice that they don't take very good care of their clothes like taking a stitch in a seam before it rips out because they have plenty more.

INTERVIEWER. I see. Is there any other way they show that they have money? You have been here a long time and have seen a lot of them, right?

ALICIA. Yes, they eat at the Crem Helado instead of going home for lunch or eating at the pensión which is much closer to CEUCA.

Interview with Helen.

INTERVIEWER. Do you find that Colombians sometimes have some stereotypes of Americans?

HELEN. Oh yes, they do! They think that all the women have loose morals and that we are "too independent"; that we are all divorced and don't like children, and to top it off we make miserable wives who want husbands to do all the housework. Another thing about Americans in general, not just the women, is that they are all rich! I wish it were true, I'd love to be rich!

INTERVIEWER. How do the Colombians get this idea that Americans are rich?

HELEN. They see a lot of American movies with cadillacs, champagne parties, and such. Then there is the advertising in the *Life en Español* which shows all of the refrigerators, cars and gadgets for sale from American companies and they give the impression that the average North American has a speedboat, deep freeze, piano, and color television. Of course there are always the American tourists who come and throw their money around at the Tequendama.

INTERVIEWER. Do you think that any of the students or Peace Corps trainees do anything to perpetuate this impression?

HELEN. There might be a few ugly Americans in the bunch but not many. I have never seen any of them do anything like that.

INTERVIEWER. Would you classify yourself as rich?

HELEN. No, but I admit I wouldn't mind being rich. I am always on a budget to scrape through college.

INTERVIEWER. Do you think that Colombians, if they knew your family's financial situation, would think of you as rich?

HELEN. Certainly, some of them would if they knew. I'm sure that the *campesinos* on the Sabana and in the Cordillera and the stevedores we saw loading the ships in Cartagena would say that I was rich just by looking at me. I wouldn't have to tell them anything.

INTERVIEWER. Right! And what about the Colombians there at CEUCA?

HELEN. Sure, the messenger-janitor or maid would think I was rich, but the others would not.

INTERVIEWER. For example, how would doña Aurora in the library or Alicia, the receptionist, view you?

HELEN. No, they wouldn't think I was rich by looking at me. They dress as well as I do. I would have to say or do something to give the impression that I had money to burn, which I don't.

INTERVIEWER. Do you think that you might have done anything to give such an impression yourself to the CEUCA staff since wealth is very relative?

HELEN. No, I have never talked to any of them about money, expenses, budgets, costs, or anything like that. All I ever talk to them about is whether a certain book has been obtained by the library, whether a message was left for me, how much postage I need on a letter going *entrega inmediata*, plus all the polite phrases such as *Buenos días, Que tenga buen fin de semana*, and that sort of stuff.

INTERVIEWER. Do you recall anything that happened yesterday that might have given the staff the impression that you specifically are rich in their own standards?

HELEN. No. Actually, I was lamenting the fact that I was *broke* after my weekend at Cartagena. I certainly could not afford to do that every weekend. Besides, I was not telling this to any of the Colombian staff but just to Margie who had also been on a weekend jaunt.

123

We should not righteously assume that a person who gives the impression of being rich is an "ugly American" type who is especially insensitive to the feelings of others. Instead, it seems more realistic and fruitful to think of this case as illustrating a common problem found in the communication between the more affluent and the less affluent. The less affluent tend to be less vocal but not necessarily less observant, while the more affluent tend to express themselves without getting any feedback from the less affluent until some crisis provokes it.

There is a tendency for the person in subordinate status to be socially "invisible" to the superordinate person. This is behind Helen's remark, "I was not telling this to any of the Colombian staff but just to my friend Margie." The focus of Helen's attention is upon the other principal actor in the scene while she was quite unconscious of the "invisible" audience. In this illustration the American seemed to assume that since she had not *directly told* any Colombians about her financial situation that they, therefore, did not know anything about it.

This illustrates the general tendency for people to be aware of their own financial limitations. They are reluctant to think of themselves as rich as long as there are others richer or if their level of aspiration runs ahead of their finances. Thus, Helen thought of the fact that she had to budget and that after her trip to Cartagena she was "broke."

From Alicia's point of view Helen *was* rich. Alicia was the same age as Helen, had not been to college but had gone to a secretarial school, then to the U.S. binational center over a period of a year to become a bilingual secretary. She was still going to night school and worked on weekends to earn extra money. She gave about 25 percent of her salary to her mother for board and room, and her monthly salary was just equal to what Helen had spent on airfare, hotel, and "mad money" on her recent two-day jaunt. Helen was not aware of this great contrast because she felt that, since the secretaries and librarian always dressed neatly and fashionably, they must have spent considerable money on clothes. Actually, Alicia's mother made some of her clothes, and Alicia made some on a borrowed sewing machine. Alicia was also very cheerful, on the surface at least, and never complained of being "broke."

Similar illustrations could be marshalled to show how the American is judged as rich because he has an expensive camera and takes many colored pictures, often with film he brought from the U.S. The impression is made more dramatic because the Colombian thinks in terms of much higher cost of this same film in Colombia.

Similarly, the simple remark, "My family in the States has two cars," might instantly put the American in the rich class in the eyes of the

Colombian who thinks of automobiles in a different light because there is a 250 percent import tax on autos in Colombia. For the *bogotano* middle class, a car is not such an absolute necessity as for many Americans who could not get to work; go shopping; and take the children to school, music lessons, friends' houses, and such, without a car. Much more of the U.S. economy is now organized upon the assumption that every family has at least one car. It is no longer a luxury item for Americans but a necessity for social and economic survival, even for the lower class.

The Colombian might overhear the American saying that he pays 30 pesos for lunch every day, but the Colombian might pay only seven. The American might never have seen any place where lunch (including soup, meat, vegetable, rolls, dessert, and coffee) could be purchased for less than 25 pesos, yet few office workers would pay more than 10. They would prefer to go home for lunch, riding the bus a half hour each way but paying only one peso for the round trip.

The American, who does not pay his share of sociable expenses while being perceived as rich, can be quickly put into the selfish category by the Colombian who sees his behavior in a different perspective. He is not always inclined to interpret the American's reluctance to pay as a result of cross-cultural confusion. He tends to impute the same motives to the American as he would to a Colombian in the same situation.

In an attempt to measure the amount of miscommunication regarding the sharing of expenses, we presented the hypothetical situation to both the Colombian señoras and American guests and asked who should pay. The situation chosen was one that was fairly common and involved a señora and her *gringa* guest taking a taxi together.

A larger proportion of the señoras (77 percent) than of the American guests (64 percent) thought the American girl should pay under the circumstances. If it had been an American boy the señoras would have been much more unanimous in agreeing that he should pay. The reasons given for expecting the American girls to pay were that it was doing her a favor to help her shop, and the girl was the one to suggest a taxi; therefore she should pay for it.

The reasons given by the señoras who expected the Colombian to pay were, "She is a member of the family," "The girl doesn't have much money," and "You have to be polite to a foreign guest."

Perhaps the reason for the larger proportion of Americans choosing to "take turns from store to store" is that they looked upon this as an application of the "Dutch treat" principle to sharing taxi fares. All but a few of the señoras avoided this solution and preferred to have the American pay or took a more *noblesse oblige* position of paying for the taxi even though the girl did suggest the whole thing. The proportion of Americans who thought the girl should pay might have been smaller if we had asked only the girls to respond to this question.

In another hypothetical case the *gringa* goes with the family on a long weekend trip.

It would be difficult for the American guest to do the correct thing in the eyes of the Colombians on the basis of information from another American living in a different home because all of the señoras did not agree.

There was a wide range of agreement among the hosts, depending upon the particular expense involved. The greatest amount of agreement (93 percent) was that the *gringa* should not pay for the gasoline; 71 percent agreed that she should not buy presents for all members of the family; 70 percent agreed that she should not pay for her room and meals at the hotel; 64 percent agreed that she should not pay all of her own expenses; and 56 percent agreed that she should offer to pay sometimes when they eat out. A majority (ranging from 56 to 93 percent) of the Colombians agreed on these five points, but on only one of these points (not paying for gasoline) did a majority of the American guests agree!

The proportion of the Americans choosing the response, "It depends," was about four times as great as for Colombians. The comments by both guests and hosts indicated that to the Americans "it depends" simply meant that they did not know what to expect because they were unable to specify what it depended upon.

One of the specified conditions that tended to increase the proportion of señoras who felt the American should pay was, "The host family *usually* goes to *Villa de Leiva* for Easter." The family probably would have taken the trip with only the immediate family or close relatives if the American had not been living with them. Also, since the guest in this case is a *gringa* some of the señoras were reluctant to allow her to stay at home while the family was away even though the live-in maid stayed in the house. So, in a sense, the *gringa* might unwittingly obligate the family to invite her to join their traditional Easter outing which would increase the expenses considerably.

In contrast, the fact that the American is a girl makes the family feel more obligated to pay all of her expenses since they think of females as being more economically dependent.

The most frequently mentioned criterion in the señora's decision was whether the *gringa* "was invited or just taken." To the Colombian there is an important and clear distinction between going with someone and being invited to go as a guest. Those who assumed that the

American was "just being taken" thought she should pay for part or all of the added expenses (therefore not the gasoline) of the trip. Those who thought she had been invited as their guest felt she should not pay for anything.

The second silent assumption had to do with "who could best afford to pay." Since the role of the American guest in the home is somewhat ambiguous with regard to whether she is a boarder, member of the family, or long-term guest, the relative ability of the family versus the *gringa* to pay became relevant. Thus, the more affluent families were more willing to pay all of the expenses, while the poorer families would be less inclined to pay. Also the apparent ability of the American to pay was a complementary factor.

The American guests who got along better with their families seemed to be those who had gained some insight into the following points:

There were certain situations in which the family felt *obligated* to take the guest along, particularly on out-of-town overnight trips. This seemed to be particularly true if the guest was a *gringa*. This represented an additional expense to the family which would not be covered by the room and board fee paid by the guest. It was wise to have a clear idea of what these additional expenses were and to offer to pay them. If he could not afford it, he should express his regrets explaining why. This gives the family the choice of saying that they intended to pay all of the expenses or to suggest some degree of sharing. If the family is not in a position to pay any of the expenses, they can accept the guest's excuse with regrets. If there were some anxiety about the guest (particularly the *gringa*) staying at the house overnight without the family, the guest might suggest staying with another host family for that period. Even if the family shows that they intend to pay all of the expenses, the guest should offer to reciprocate in some way on the trip or afterwards. For example, he could pay for the meal when they all eat out. As inconvenient as it may seem to the American, he needs to find ways of avoiding the "Dutch treat" approach by reciprocating or by taking the initiative.

Americans might be more reluctant to pay their share when abroad for some of the following reasons.

Linguistic ineptness. Sometimes the American simply does not understand the full significance of certain words and will think he is invited as a guest when he is not, or he will invite someone else as his guest when he has no intention to do so.

Insecurity. In the newness of the foreign situation and with the problems of bridging the culture gap, some Americans begin to feel insecure and tend to compensate by retreating to a more dependent relationship than they would have with their own family in the United States. They tend to think of the phrase, "They treat me like a member of the family," as being treated as his own parents treated him when he was 14 years old, because while abroad he sometimes needs some of the same kind of support. We have noted that some hosts were often puzzled by the apparent inconsistency in the American who wants adult freedoms and privileges in some ways while being so dependent in others.

Lack of knowledge. The American is often caught off guard because he does not know when and where to expect which obligations. He may not know far enough in advance to be prepared to pay his share of the expenses, nor does he know when and how to reciprocate when he has incurred obligations.

Budgetary pressures. A person who would be quite willing to pay his share of the expenses in the States suddenly becomes tight-fisted when he is abroad because he wants to make the most of his "one and only" opportunity in the foreign country by traveling on weekends and vacations to see and do as many things as possible. In addition, there was the acute problem of rapidly obtaining additional funds from the United States if he ran over his budgeted spending money. Therefore, many of the American students obtained part-time jobs teaching English or working in travel bureaus or other establishments where they could use their bilingual skill in order to be able to do the things they wanted to do during vacation breaks.

Lack of identification. It was clear that in a few cases the American did not identify with (or have enough empathy with) Colombians strongly enough to care whether they thought of him as a "tightwad" or not. This is consistent with the data we gave showing that a large proportion of the Colombians felt that the Americans "didn't care about their reputation among Colombians." In a sense, this was a breakdown of the ordinary social obligations which would have moved the American to be more generous among his acquaintances in the United States.

Cross-Cultural "Bobbing"

We are all familiar with one "bobbing" situation within our own culture when two persons simultaneously passing through a doorway in opposite directions try to guess which side the other one is going to take. Then each "bobs" to the left and right in such a way as to unintentionally block the other.

This same reciprocal miscalculation occurs between the North American and the Latin American when each tries to calculate the other's behavior in terms of the other's cultural background. Thus, the American tries to pay the whole check while the Colombian tries to let him go "Dutch treat."[6] Or the Colombian knowing the American's reputation for punctuality might inform him that a party will begin at 10:00 p.m. instead of announcing it formally for 9:00; then the American, knowing that parties do not begin at the announced time, will allow an hour and arrive at 11:00 p.m. In the meantime the Colombian assumes that the American is not going to come since he did not arrive on time. Or a Colombian selling fresh vegetables in the street market might have learned that the North American is always in a hurry and has little patience with "bargaining" when buying produce; so when the North American asks the price, the merchant immediately gives his "selling price" rather than his "asking price" to save time. Then the North American, knowing that it is customary to bargain over fresh produce, tries to persuade the seller to lower the price still further.

Needless to say, there are many specific forms of cross-cultural bobbing, some humorous, some sad, some exhilarating, some tedious, and some downright dangerous as in the case of bobbing between two drivers or between a pedestrian and a car. Whether there is more cross-cultural bobbing when each knows something of the other's customs or when neither knows anything of the other's customs is hard to guess, but it is clear that bobbing is at a minimum if the American knows the Colombian's customs and the Colombian knows nothing of the American customs.

The Gringo's Feet

One thing that prevented the North American from being whole-heartedly accepted as a member of the family was one he often considered an "unimportant detail." He had a difficult time understanding the strength of the *bogotano's* reaction to the "offensive use of his feet."

The *gringo's* feet tended to offend the host's sensitivities in two ways. He shocked the host by running around the house barefoot, and when he did have shoes on, he was putting his feet on sofas, coffee tables, chairs, beds, and other furniture. These irritating events were not very frequent, but they left a strong negative impression on the señora. It is difficult in print to convey the feeling which came through so clearly in the tone of voice in the taperecorded interviews.

> I have only known foreigners from the United States. These boys are serious boys but of course their general culture or manners do not impress me very much. For example, they sit down and put their feet on top of the chairs!

Ben was completely North American, very typical. Well, he was from Texas. Yes, he was a little rough, more friendly than many. He would come here to the house to study with Richard. He would put his feet on top of the coffee table. He wasn't very refined but he was a very intelligent boy.

When Bill first came, he would not polish his shoes for about a week. So I told him that he should polish them. I asked him if he didn't feel embarrassed to go to the university with dirty shoes. He said he had not brought any polish, so I told him to buy some and keep his shoes shiny.

I understand that it is not just the younger generation North Americans who put their feet on top of things all the time. I saw a movie where the hero who was a detective put his feet up on his own desk while talking to a police woman. Then I saw another one where the boss in this business office always put his feet on the desk right in front of his secretary. Since I don't believe everything I see in the movies I began asking some North Americans here whether that is a custom of respectable people in the United States and they said that it does happen.

It is very strange, they seem to think they are in outer space or for some reason they don't know up from down. They seem to like their feet up and their head down!

All but one of the above comments by the hosts are referring to male guests. Apparently the female guests seldom offended the Colombians in this way.

The North Americans failed to comprehend the essential nature of Colombian social norms. Following are reactions of two North Americans to the information that their señora was shocked by their behavior.

I have done that *only once* in the living room, and in my own bedroom that is only my business.

Yes, I suspected that they wouldn't like it, but after all I *didn't do it every day*. Just a couple of times after I had been out walking all over the town and my feet were tired. It feels good to get them up!

They seemed to think it strange that the señora's reaction was out of proportion to the frequency with which they committed the act. The point that is missed is that, if a certain action is taboo, a person needs to do it only once (like standing on the altar of the church during communion) to be immediately put into a special category as a type of deviant who is capable of such an act. In some of the *bogotanos'* minds this act was clearly interpreted as an act to assert one's superiority.

Going barefooted in the wrong places was more prevalent than putting shod feet on the furniture. In general, the *bogotano* hosts seemed to object to the bare feet because they thought of it as a dirty habit. Some of the North Americans came from colleges where students go barefooted on the street, in the classroom, in local restaurants, cafeterias, and student hangouts. For some this is such an important symbol of freedom that they will go barefooted outdoors when the temperature is in the 40s and 50s, which involves some discomfort. Other North Americans were not accustomed to going barefooted outside their own home or dormitory but thought it perfectly permissible inside the home. Here are some of the hosts' reactions to bare feet in their homes.

> The North Americans are always walking around barefooted and of course their feet get dirty. So the next time you have to change the towels because they are very dirty. I think they clean their dirty feet on the towels. I told him not to do this because one day I caught him drying his feet with the hand towel, so I told him the towel was for the hands, *not* for the feet. It was embarrassing for me to have to tell him this; it is not pleasant scolding him.

> It is a problem the way they take their shoes off and walk around barefooted, so I've told them I know it is a custom in the United States, but not here. . . . I considered this to be a bad example for my children. I don't know whether they liked it, but they accepted and followed my advice.

> She always has such dirty feet. For example, one Saturday she went out to the country and she came in with her feet full of mud and she bathed a few times and when a week later I saw her feet they were still dirty. I told her she had no right to keep her feet that way. I recommended that she use some salt soap and some pumice stone and wash them well.

Sometimes when the señora tried to correct the North American's behavior, she would take an indirect approach.

> I told him that he was liable to catch cold or even pneumonia walking in the hall barefooted. They always complain about the cold here in Bogotá but won't even put on slippers to go to the bathroom.

> Donald always walked around the house in his bare feet and I was afraid he would embarrass some of my friends; so one day I told him that it was dangerous to walk around the house barefooted because of the wooden floors. There are slivers and sometimes pieces of broken glass in the dining room because the maid is always breaking glasses and dishes. But he just said, "Don't worry about me, I have tough feet, I'm used to it!"

> I don't think he realizes how the bottoms of his feet look with them up on a chair as he studies in his room. That's not a pretty sight to treat your friends to when they come to see you. I finally told him that when a person is studying his circulation slows down and there is danger that he will catch cold if he doesn't wear shoes or slippers. I should have told him that it also gets his sheets all dirty down below because he can't get his feet clean.

Some señoras used the indirect approach illustrated above; others took a more direct approach; many of them simply suffered in silence and hoped their friends would not see their guest in his bare feet. Luckily, most of the señora's friends would visit in the afternoon before the guest returned home from the day's activities. Otherwise more of the señoras would have felt impelled to correct their guest. In some instances it was the señor's remark that stimulated the señora to say something to the guest. The unpleasant task of correcting the guest's behavior usually fell to the señora.

Even after the North American guests had lived with a *bogotano* family for periods ranging from three to six months, they still did not realize the extent of the families' objections to going barefooted in the home. The señoras were asked if their guests could be barefooted in each of five situations in the home. The guests overestimated the number of señoras who would approve (except "in living room visiting friend" when all of the female guests correctly thought that none of the señoras would approve).

The symbolic value of walking around barefooted is very different in the Latin American middle-class culture than it has become in the North American middle-class student subculture. To the *bogotano* bare feet on the floor or ground are not associated with intellectual freedom, youth, and spontaneity. Instead, the association is with the ignorance, poverty and unsanitary conditions of the poorest *campesino*. Even the *campesino* usually tries to have something on his feet even if only homemade sandals with soles of rubber tire treads. It certainly is not the "intellectual" thing to do, nor is it associated with freedom since only the lowest class goes barefoot when forced by economic necessity or when ignorant of the relationship between going barefoot and certain diseases they contract. Thus, a person would not go barefoot by choice unless he wanted to shock or insult those about him.

In the eyes of the host families the North American guest who goes barefoot in the house or puts his feet on the furniture is not acting "like a member of the family." The lack of awareness of the guests to the señoras' objections has several partial explanations: In some families the college-aged guest had no role model to observe since there were no children at home; when he did observe that the Colombian children did not go barefoot he could simply assume that to wear shoes or not is a manner of personal choice since no one verbally corrected the guest; when the señora felt she had to say something, her suggestion was not understood because it was too indirect; and some of the señoras did not try to correct the guest because they were either trying to be accepting of different customs or, on the basis of previous attempts to correct a particular North American, they felt he would not accept any correction. In any case, the overall effect is to create a barrier to communication between the North American guests and the Colombian family.

Notes

1. The data for this section are based on a questionnaire designed and administered by Miss Hermena W. Evans who was in charge of housing the CEUCA students with Colombian families in Bogotá.
2. For example, the New Englander is much less likely to shake hands than the Texan. The New Englander's pattern is more like that in England today, while the Texan's is more like that of the Mexican or Colombian.
3. The use of the *abrazo* and styles in between the standard handshake and the *abrazo* such as men grasping the other's upper arm or shoulder with the left hand while shaking with the right have not been discussed.
4. Some thought of "Good evening" as meaning hello and "Good night" as meaning goodbye.
5. *Detallista* is probably a *colombianismo* when used in this sense. In many Spanish–English dictionaries it is defined as "a retailer, a detailer, a person fond of detail."
6. Sometimes any possibility of confusion over who is going to pay the check at the restaurant is neatly avoided by the Colombian who uses the following *bogotano* tactic. He excuses himself from the table before the last course when the check arrives. He then goes to the cashier, asks for the check, pays it and returns to the table without mentioning his mission. The other person waits for the check which never comes, and if he asks the waiter for it he is informed that it has already been paid.

8

The Guest's Relationship with Specific Family Members

Although many of the guest's problems could involve the señora, none of them were mainly her problem. There were, however, several facets of the North American's activities in the family that did mainly involve interaction with the señora. She often acted as an intermediary between the guest and the husband, the maid, the children (except those of the same age and sex as the guest), relatives, friends, and neighbors. In view of this central position of the señora, getting along well with her is tantamount to getting along well with the family.

The Señora

The policies of the different programs placing Americans in Colombian homes varied somewhat with regard to the degree to which the American guest was to be treated like a Colombian son or daughter. The variations were small in comparison to the common general policy of requiring the guest to adapt to the host culture. Regardless of the policy of the particular program, the señoras tended to act independently upon their own judgment in their treatment of the Americans. For this reason there was more variation from one host family to another within the same program than there was between programs.

The señora as a supervisor

Most of the señoras needed no urging to persuade them to treat the American, particularly a female, like a member of the family with respect to exercising some supervision over their activities. The señora did not supervise the *gringa* because that was what she was paid to do. The anxiety she sometimes suffered could not be purchased with money. Her willingness to supervise the guest sprang from three main sources. First, as a parent she has developed all of the reflexes associated with that role. She automatically felt responsible for the American guest, particularly if she already had children of that age. Her conscience impelled her to see that the guest behaved correctly. Some of the señoras were able to relax this super-ego to some degree because they felt that the American was from a different culture accustomed to more freedom or that the American girls had no virginity to protect.

Second, the señora's concern for harmony and solidarity among all of the members of her household made her sensitive to any of the guest's behavior that might create dissension among household members. If the guest's behavior set a bad example for her own children and caused them to clamor for more privileges, she would be caught in the middle of the controversy and would have to make a choice between relaxing the supervision of her own child or tightening up the supervision of her American guest.

Third, where a señora had no children, she was still subjected to social pressure to make the American guest conform to the cultural pattern. It was important to the señora to have a good reputation in the community. She did not want to take the blame for actions actually committed by her guest, nor did she want to be accused of allowing her home to be used as a haven for some type of deviant behavior. She had to keep a reputation of running a respectable home and had to demonstrate that she was in command of the situation. The señoras expressed considerable genuine anxiety about the welfare of the American guest when asked, "In what ways might an American guest worry you more (and worry you less) than your own son or daughter of the same age?"

Yes, one of the girls worried me more than my own daughter. One time she was sick and I was very sorry for her. With the second one I didn't know where she was. She wouldn't let me know. I told her about it and one time even called CEUCA and told them that I'd like for her to let me know where she was and at what time she was returning but she would never do it.

Well, I was very worried about Robin . . . that something would happen to her. I would have been responsible and it would be very, very serious if something had happened while she was in my house. She worried me more than my own daughter would because, when she wanted to do something foolish, I couldn't say no. Like the time she wanted to go to Cartagena with some boys and sleep overnight on the beach. I told her not to go but she went anyway.

I was always worried about them getting sick. . . . You know how to treat your own children but you are afraid to give any medicine to these students. I also feared when they stayed out at night without letting me know . . . that something had happened. From the very first day they came I told them to always let me know if they were going to be in late, but sometimes they forgot.

They worry me more than my own child because they are shy and might not ask for something they need like some medicine . . . or they might not like the food but won't say anything.

Yes, it worries me in the sense that he is a foreigner and could have had problems and I do not want him to have a bad impression of the family.

I would worry much more than with my own children because you should worry more about things that are not yours than your own personal things.

To me it is a big problem when the girls stayed out late at night, you know. I worry about what a big problem I would have if one of these girls became pregnant. They know how to deal with their own boys in the States but with these it is very difficult. I worry much more about them when they are with Colombian boys than with American boys.

They can worry me more than my own children when they get ill. I would be terrified for them to get sick because that's a very big responsibility. I would go crazy if this happened to us. I'm with my husband and children and I'm in my own country, but if anything happens to the American girls you would call your doctor, but that worries me.

They worry me more because of their ways of acting familiar with the boys . . . not that I am worried about her morals but because it is setting a bad example for my children.

Having a *gringa* in your home is a very delicate situation. It's the same thing when someone leaves a baby in the house which is not yours. You leave everything aside to take care of that baby because it is a great responsibility!

I have not had any problems with my own daughters because they are obedient. . . . So you worry more about a person you don't know well enough because she may not respond to advice.

Some señoras found some aspects of behavior less problematical with the Americans than with their own children of the same age.

Well, you would worry a lot about your own children being successful in school or college, but if the North American comes here and doesn't study it doesn't worry you.

They worry me less because I don't have to form their moral sentiments. They have already formed their morals. They are grown up when they arrive here. I would worry about my son if his ideas were different and he didn't have the idea that the family was important for him.

With your own daughter you are worried about her virginity, but with the *gringa* she has already lost that!

When my daughter went to Javeriana University I would not let her come home alone after 7:00 p.m. but would go in the car to pick her up, but with the *gringas* I have no such worries because I know that they have been trained to greater independence.

The señora as advisor

We found that the señora was the most important person in giving daily advice to the American guest, next was some Colombian peer (such as a student of the same sex at the university attended by the American), and third was anyone directly associated with the sponsoring American organization.

Since the señora probably has more to lose than any other person associated with the American if he does not live up to certain minimum standards of adjustment to the culture, she is highly motivated to give advice spontaneously. The American frequently asks her for advice.

The most salient category of advice was on relations with the opposite sex. Most of this advice was given to the female guests and was given three times as often as it was asked for by the guest. The issue was very important in the minds of the señoras. Security precautions cover advice on protecting oneself against theft, robbery, assault, traffic accidents, and disease. Along with manners, these were the major areas of advice given by host families.

It is one thing to say that advice was given and quite another to say that the advice was heeded. Sometimes the people in the agency sponsoring the Americans in Bogotá would become so involved in the problem cases of the Americans who would not take advice (or who used techniques to obtain the type of advice they wanted to hear) that they would fail to wonder why so many of these young Americans did take advice. Ordinarily, we might not think that this would merit any special explanation. But in view of the fact that many of the Americans left United States campuses in a somewhat rebellious mood and that much of the advice represented a restriction on the Americans' freedom, some explanation seems called for.

Source of emotional support. Some of the señoras noted that American guests were "easier to handle" than a Colombian university student who was not a relative would be because "They are unsure of themselves," "They don't know the ropes yet," or "They are open to suggestion." Under the conditions of cultural immersion, the same person who might be proving his independence from his own parents and from other forms of the establishment feels the need for some support from a family group while abroad. One very significant indicator of the guest's acceptance of the host family is in the terminology used to designate its members. In a majority of the interviews with the Americans they referred to the señora as "my mother," to the Colombian son as "my brother" and the daughter as "my sister." Also interesting is the fact that the possessive "my" was dropped in talking about "the aunt," "the cousin," and "the grandfather." Thus, under the stress of cultural immersion the host family represents a source of psychological support that gives it more influence than it would have if this support were not needed.

Doorkeeper of the culture. The need for emotional support is quite different from the need for information which can also be fulfilled by the host family as a doorkeeper of the culture. When the American first arrives in Colombia, it is abundantly evident to all but the most insensitive that he is in a foreign culture. As he has more direct interaction with the Colombians, he realizes that these people have no intention of conforming to his ways; then he realizes that they are all part of a system that cannot be thrown out of step for the foreign visitor. Also, for some it is painful to recognize that it does no good to protest or to complain because there is no audience among the Colombians who can give sympathy or even understand the complaint. Under these conditions the choice is either to learn how to participate, withdraw into social isolation, or seek the company of one's compatriots. Those who choose to conform are much more likely to ask for advice, more likely to follow it and, therefore, more likely to inspire the señora to volunteer advice that they do not yet know they need. The American in the foreign culture realizes that the host family did not invent the culture merely to ram it down his throat. Instead, he views the family as people with the practical knowledge to help him solve problems he meets in his new environment.

The challenge of the new and exotic. The idea of presenting a challenge of adapting to something new seems to be effective particularly with budding intellectuals. This helps to account for why some advice is accepted and some rejected in the communication between the same two people, because not everything encountered in the foreign culture is exotic. If the idea is a familiar one in the United States, particularly among members of the older generation, the North American student is often more resistant to the advice that is then "old hat," "old fashioned," or "what my grandmother would tell me." The advice with a familiar ring to the American may trigger the particular reflexes toward the "conservative establishment" he has learned in his own culture.

This tendency to accept the challenge of the exotic and to reject the old-fashioned ideas is shown in the following example of the same American girl asking the same Colombian señora for advice on two different occasions. In the first instance she happily accepted the advice, and in the second instance she automatically rejected it. This is told from the point of view of the American.

> I knew that there was going to be some very special religious celebration on the Day of the Immaculate Conception and that it was going to be a big thing here in Bogotá. Being from Protestant background I didn't have the foggiest notion of what it was about, so I thought I would ask my mother. She explained that this was celebrating the day when the Virgin Mary found out that she had conceived and that it was God's child. Of course I had never celebrated this in the United States so she described the special Mass that would be said in all the churches and how lilies would be used in the services to symbolize purity. I asked if I could attend a mass and she told me just what to do and everything, so I did it, and it was very interesting!

> We had this party on Saturday night and I was the only *gringa* there. We mainly danced and had drinks. The girls didn't drink very much but the boys, some of them, drank quite a bit. Some of them seem to be afraid of girls until they have a little to drink and then they are just the opposite. Anyway, I danced with eight or ten boys during the evening and they were just a bunch of wolves. They would get you in the corner and press up against you in a way that wasn't exactly dancing. One of them got just a little fresh the first time I danced with him and then the second time he got so bad that right in the middle of the dance floor I walked off and left him. I had gotten enough of that stuff. He just seemed to think that all of the *gringas* are easy to get because I had never seen him before that night. I had decided that I wasn't going to go to any more parties if they were all like this one. I went to one before but there were three or four American boys there . . . so if one of the *colombianos* got too fresh I would just ask one of the Americans to dance.

> Anyway, I told my mother about this problem and that I was thinking about not going to any more parties where there was dancing. I wanted her to tell me how to keep these wolves under control, but she told me that the way she did it was to never let your legs touch theirs and to put your hand on the front of his shoulder so that you can push gently to keep him at the right distance. Well, I was asking for advice but I didn't want to hear any of that "Grandma Perkins" advice about how she did it. I think the only thing to do is to tell them off if they get fresh or just walk away and leave them standing alone.

Actually, in the second situation the American was lucky to have a señora who would be so clearly explicit in giving practical advice which was essentially correct. The girl was not having these difficulties because of a stereotype of *gringas* obtained from movies from the United States but because this particular *gringa* was using her body in a way which means something very different to the *colombiano* than to the American college student. She was in fact signaling to the Colombian that she was indeed interested in more than dancing.

In spite of the correctness of the advice, the *gringa* instantaneously rejected it because she thought it was the outdated idea of a particular old

139

lady. She did not realize that the vast majority of the señoras in the host families would agree with the advice given.

Restrictiveness of norms. Another variable that seemed to determine the probability of the guest's acceptance of the advice was the degree to which the advice tended to restrict the American's choice of behaviors. The more restrictive, the less likely the guest was to accept it. For example, if they asked what they should wear on a picnic, the señora would tell them that they could wear a dress or slacks if they wanted, so wearing the slacks in this case would not be a rejection of the advice. However, if the girl asked what she could wear on a trip downtown and the señora said either a suit or a dress, then the girl who had hoped to wear slacks would feel that the suggestion was restrictive and might decide to reject it. Similarly, if the girl who had asked what to wear at the picnic had been hoping to wear shorts, the idea of slacks would have been restrictive and, therefore, less likely to be heeded.

Value potency. When the señoras gave advice on things that were not merely a matter of taste but more clearly a case of morality, there was a tendency for the señora to be more emphatic and for the guest to accept the advice.

Survival value. If the advice was obviously important to the American's material well being, physical safety, or social status, it was more likely to be heeded than if it were not.

The advice on material and physical aspects was effective from the beginning of the stay, but it took some time for the American to be integrated into Colombian circles firmly enough for him to care what his status might be in any particular group of Colombians. We noted cases where the guest readily accepted advice which would help him behave appropriately in a group of his peers, but rejected advice on how to get along with professors or other older adults he contacted frequently. In some cases the American acted as if older Colombian adults were invisible.

Since the señora tended to mention only the more dramatic types of advice that had high value potency for her and high survival value for the guest, a large proportion of this reported advice was accepted. But when we more directly asked the señoras if they thought that Amercian guests in general accepted advice (and did not let them give specific examples of the advice they had personally given to their own guests), the señoras were much more ambivalent. Forty-five percent disagreed with the statement, "They do *not* accept advice."

This discrepancy may be due in part to the difference between the señoras' responses to a general stereotype of the "willful and spoiled *gringo*" and their responses regarding the particular *gringo* they had as a guest in their own home. It might also be due to the *gringos'* tendency to accept the more salient types of advice. We feel that both factors were operating in the minds of the señoras.

Acceptable ways to help the señora

Very frequently the American guests would point out the problem of returning favors that the host family had done for them. Often they are not sure how to pay their share; they realize this and want to reciprocate in some way. In some cases the American's attempt to reciprocate happened to be in a form not appreciated by the Colombians. For example, here are some attempts at reciprocation which the Americans thought were not successful.

> I wanted to do something nice for the family because they had taken me to a *fútbol* game, a bullfight, to the *Quinta de Bolívar*, and to the Colón theater, and to parties. So I took their three boys, ages 9, 11, and 13, to the *vespertina* movie one Sunday. I should say that I offered to take them, but the father objected and wouldn't let me do it. I was talking to the kids on Saturday afternoon about going the next day. I don't know why he objected. It was clear that he didn't approve of the idea.

In this case the problem was that the father felt that his children should not develop a taste for movies on both Saturday and Sunday, and previously they had always gone on Saturday. Probably more important was the fact that Sundays were the best opportunities for the father to enjoy his three sons whom he rarely saw during the week since they ate breakfast after he left for work and had already eaten dinner before the father arrived home at night.

> We had a terrific dinner party at our house and it was a lot of trouble for the maid and the señora to get everything ready. So after the guests had left, I thought I would give the maid a little help. I know that usually husbands (or maybe men in general) do not usually do dishes and that sort of thing, but I just thought I would give a boost to help them out. I could tell that something was deeply disturbing the maid when I went into the kitchen with a tray full of dishes; then when the señora came in I knew I had done something wrong.

In this case the problem was that a *male* guest had invaded the kitchen. There may have been some other way he could have helped, but the sight of a man in the kitchen trying to help scrape the dishes was too disturbing to the social status and was more distracting than helpful.

> At home I was used to mowing the lawn and keeping the garden in shape . . . also I felt the need for some exercise which is a real problem here because the university does not have gym classes, there is no swimming pool, and I don't

have a bicycle here, so all the exercise I get is walking and chasing buses. Anyway, I got the bright idea I would do my family a favor by fixing up the garden which usually was in great shape. Now, was that ridiculous! First, I found that they had no lawn mower. At that time I had not noticed that the gardener came on Wednesday mornings and cut it with a pair of hand shears. It's a good thing the lawn is so small! Well, since there wasn't any lawn mower I wasn't going to be stopped completely so I got a hand trowel and was taking out the weeds around the roses. That did it, you would think that I had committed some major crime the way my mother came out screaming at me not to "dig around the plants." It's pretty hard to find anything you can do to reciprocate for favors they have done.

This American was right that it is particularly difficult for the male guest to find some active way to help to reciprocate for favors received, unless he is alert to try to share expenses when that is permissible and to pay the whole check part of the time in situations where sharing is not customary. The only acceptable way discovered by some of the American male guests was in making minor repairs in such things as doorbells or leaky faucets. Although the Colombian señor might not do these things, the señora is very pleased if the American student will do it. However, many of the students did not have enough experience to be more of a help than a hazard in such undertakings.[1]

Of course the female guest has many more ways of reciprocating for favors received from the family. This is fortunate, since the families were more inclined to do favors for and pay the expenses of the female than of the male guest.

In addition to the regular daily chores expected of the guests in caring for their own rooms, beds, clothes, towels and personal items, there are many ways she can reciprocate for favors done by the family and to build rapport with the señora:

1. Keeping own room neat.[2]
2. Teaching English to family members.
3. Arranging house for a party.
4. Buying things for a party.
5. Preparing a special dinner for a party.
6. Helping with housework when there is no maid.
7. Setting table for dinner party.
8. Taking care of younger children.
9. Sweeping own room.

The mere knowledge that a certain type of help would be appreciated is not always enough to assure us that this help will be given. Even if the guests' actions lived up to their own perceptions of the señoras' expectations, many of the guests would be found wanting by the señoras.

For example, teaching English to family members is something that 71 percent of the Colombians feel the American should offer to do. Not only did the guests fall short of perceiving this desire, but also among those who did perceive it there was considerable resistance to the idea and practically none of them ever tried it.

> I think that a lot of the host families, including my own, would like to have us teach them some English. They may sort of hint around that their son, now in the 11th grade, has been taking English in school but he is afraid to try to speak it because his pronunciation is not very good. I think that is one reason they took a *gringo* into their home, but I'm here in Colombia to learn Spanish and I can't do that if I'm speaking English all the time. If they want to learn English, they should go to the United States, that's the only way to really learn it!

> Sometimes the señor, who is an engineer, will ask me what a certain word means in a book he is reading in English, or he will ask me for the English equivalent of a Spanish word. I don't mind this but I don't like to spend too much time talking about English.

> I know that my mother would like me to teach some English to the 10 and 12 year old girls in our house, but I don't have the foggiest notion how to go about it if I wanted to. Sometimes I greet them in English and they do the same with me, but that is not teaching them the language. Sometimes I feel a little guilty because I know that my mother and father do correct my Spanish from time to time and give some of the vocabulary I need. But they understand that I am here to learn Spanish and to learn about Colombia, so they don't really expect me to teach the girls English.

This reluctance to become involved with teaching English to any host-family members may seem inconsistent with the fact that about 25 percent of the guests at some time during their stay applied for a job teaching English at some special center in Bogotá. About half of these people actually taught English over a period of time. The pay ranged from nothing to board and room or $3 per class hour. Most of them taught at the Centro Colombo-Americano or the Meyer Language Center.

The one obvious difference between teaching at the latter center and teaching a family member is that the Center pays $3 per hour, while the family would usually not expect to pay. However, there are other important differences. The American fears that there may be no limit on the demands made by the family once he begins to teach any one member, while teaching at any center in Bogotá has clear limitations and a predictable schedule. Teaching at a center also often provides an opportunity to meet Colombians he would not otherwise meet. In addition, working with a class under institutional auspices provides a kind of recognition that would not be forthcoming for teaching members of the host family. Finally, in the institutional settings the American receives some training and is supplied with special materials to be used with a group in the classroom, while the guest who tries to do something with the family is thrown upon his own resources.

The argument that it will interfere with the American's learning Spanish is not very persuasive in view of the fact that sometimes the same person who gave this reason spent several hours per week watching American movies with Spanish subtitles.

The female guest should at least offer to help in preparation for a house party in whichever ways she feels most proficient. This is consistent with "being like a member of the family," since the señora herself and any older daughters would help in these ways. Many of the Americans did not know that their señora would appreciate an offer to help in these tasks.

The señora, of all the members of the host family, had the most communication with the American guest. More communication and more miscommunication, more harmony and more conflict arose with the señora than with any other member of the host family. Conflict was generated not only in the cases of miscommunication, but also in the cases of communication because the señora was the main agent of inducting the American into the ways of the foreign culture that conflict with the American's own cultural background. She was the one who assumed the major responsibility for supervising and advising the foreign guest in her home.

The Maid

After that with the señora, the American guest's next most problematical relationship was with the maid. The basic source of the problems was the fact that she had a role in the family for which there was no equivalent in the homes from which the Americans came. They did not understand the role of a maid in the United States much less in Colombia. Only one American among more than 100 who were studied had a maid in the United States.

The problems generated in the interaction between the maid and the American guest were mainly problems from the Colombian point of view. The American tended to gauge his relationships in terms of the presence or absence of direct conflict with a person. Therefore, relationships with social subordinates were often rated more highly than those with equals who would dare to disagree.

From the point of view of the Americans, their relations with the maids were not very problematical. In fact the data indicate that the better the American felt about his relationship with the maid, the worse it appeared to the señora.

All but one of the host families had at least one maid. In this case, there were no children at home, and the señora's maiden sister did much of the work a maid would have ordinarily done. While the American guests tend to associate having a maid with being upper class, this is clearly not the case in Bogotá where practically all of the middle-class families have a maid. Even families with an income with buying power equivalent to $5,000 in the United States had a maid.

In Bogotá the upper class (less than one percent of the population) have two or three live-in maids, plus auxiliary help of various kinds such as a cook, gardener, washwoman, seamstress, houseboy, or private guard (*portero* or *velador*). This does not mean that any family having some help in addition to the maid is necessarily upper class. They may be upper-middle class such as psychiatrists, physicians, career army officers, and business men.

Learning how to get along with the maid is important for the American guest because the maid is an extension of the señora's own ego. To fail to get along with the maid is to fail to get along with the señora.

Status of the maid

The status relationship between the maid and the family can be summarized by locating it on three relevant social dimensions. (1) The maid is not treated as an equal (or potential equal as are the children in the family) but as a subordinate. (2) She is neither friend nor enemy but is treated with affective neutrality in a polite and business-like fashion for the most part. (3) She is not an independent worker but dependent upon the paternalistic protection of the family and the Colombian law.

As long as the guest treated the maid in accordance with her status, she knew how to react. Some of the Americans thought that the maid was not treated "democratically as she should be treated" by the family.

In some of the families where the American felt the maid was mistreated, there was less consideration of the maid than in other families, but in other cases the American's feeling was based on a somewhat ethnocentric assumption that "in the United States everyone is treated alike." (In some cases the Colombian señora also seemed to be persuaded by the sincere American that this was true.) It is possible for an American, particularly from a large city in northern United States, to have the illusion that he "treats everyone alike" because of the strong tendency toward segregation of the races, ethnic groups, and social classes into different urban neighborhoods. This allows him to treat all those he meets daily in his neighborhood and school "democratically" because they all happen to be in his own social stratum. Nevertheless, only a minority of the

145

American guests would subscribe to this naive view that we do not make class distinctions in the United States or that there is in fact perfectly equal opportunity for all. Most of them clearly recognize this as an ideal.

For various reasons, a minority of the American guests, when confronted with the reality of the social class consciousness in the Colombian home, would feel that their democratic sensibilities had been violated and would react with considerable emotion.

> My father yells at the maid, "Come up here," and she asks, "What do you want?" and he shouts back, "I said come up here." So she finally goes up and then he says, "Bring me up some orange juice," instead of saying that in the first place and saving her the extra trip upstairs.

> I noticed that the maid's daughter does not join in the fun at the birthday party but stands behind the chair and watches.

> We are not supposed to talk with the maid because she's supposed to be an inferior person. I just can't get that idea through my head.

> The way my family talks about the lower classes and their attitude toward the maid shows that there are much greater class differences than I had expected. They treat her like a dog, not like she's a person. They make her bring them up a glass of water from the kitchen at 11 o'clock at night. They criticize her for doing something wrong, like she forgot to bring up my soup spoon and put it on the table. What really happened was that she put it in the wrong place on the table and somebody else had it who wasn't going to have soup. They jump on her for things like this. They tell her that she does not work hard enough, that she isn't a good cook, or she isn't working fast enough. The maid has a two-year-old son who stays in the back room where he has his box and he stays there. If he starts crying in the morning they get mad and say, "Be quiet," but if the dog barks in the afternoon and wakes up the kid, this is nothing. I think in my family is where I've seen the greatest class difference.

When some of the American guests began to try to treat the maid "democratically," they found some unanticipated consequences.

> You want to treat the maids like human beings which many of the people here don't do and this is very disgusting to me. It's hard for me to live with, so I try to counteract this but then the maid doesn't know how to react because it is so different from what she is used to.

> I was very friendly with the maid and she borrowed money from me and left the family without telling anybody!

> I didn't like the way the father treated the maid, so I felt very sorry for her. I talked to her quite a bit, so now she thinks she is my special friend. I think that this has gone a little too far now because when I'm lying on the bed reading, she'll come and lie on top of me and call me her pillow or something.

> I had been very friendly with the maid in a way she is not used to. Then she tried to get me to loan her my camera. Then she asked if I would promise not to tell the señora if she invited her boyfriend, the policeman, in the house while the señora was away. I could see that I was getting in over my head because the

señora had told me never to let any of the maid's friends in the house because they might rob it. But what was I to do if I was her friend?

Although the Americans sometimes felt the undesirable repercussions of treating the maid in a manner to which she was not accustomed, these repercussions were more frequently felt by the señoras.

> I know that in the United States, the families who have maids treat them as part of the family and even let them sit at the table with the rest of the family. But in the United States anyone could be a maid without lowering her social status so the Americans try to treat the maids here the same way. They don't know that they don't know how to read or write and that some of them have very low morals . . . so you have to maintain a certain social distance. The problem is that the students come and start to talk to the maids and the maids are not accustomed to this and think that the boys have the intention of making love to them.

One "signal" gave the Colombian maids the idea that the American males wanted to make love to them.

> It took me a while to discover why the maids either giggled or backed off when I talked to them. Before I came to Colombia I had read the *Silent Language* by Edward Hall, where he said that in Latin America the appropriate conversational distance is much closer than in the United States. He even gave an example of how the American gave the Latin American the impression that he was aloof by always backing away when the Latin American was trying to carry on a normal conversation with him. So I had made up my mind not to be stuck up and get right in there and talk, but that idea does not apply to maids, at least in Colombia. Most of them back away.

> I noticed at the Tocarema Hotel that when the maid came into the room to make the bed she backed away from me as I passed the bed to go out the door. Then when I wanted to give María, the maid at our house, some pesos to go to the store to buy something, she stayed so far away from me that it seemed like I could hardly reach across the distance to give her the money!

In both of these cases the problem was one of proxemics in which a middle-class male was trying to approach too closely to a lower-class female. The first American's idea was based upon his interpretation of Edward Hall's *Silent Language*. Actually Hall does not say whether the close conversational distance was appropriate between opposite sexes and different social classes. He merely gave one concrete example in face-to-face communication in which the North and the South American happened to be of the same sex and social class. Unfortunately, the student overgeneralized from the example in trying to apply it to his own conversation with the Colombian maid.

The señoras' more general complaint, that the Americans did not maintain the appropriate status difference with the maid, appeared repeatedly in the interviews.

> In general the North Americans are not proud. They treat the maids well. Very, very well in fact. They treat them as if they are equals. Sometimes it is a little upsetting because we are not used to that. There should be a balance precisely because of the social difference. Here we have to know how to behave with the different categories of people. If you try to explain to the Americans they don't understand because they come from such a different culture background.

> I don't let the Americans speak to the maid because they don't know how to handle them. They don't understand the situation. They don't know what a maid is. They don't know how to tell them. They don't understand that we have them to serve us. For example, the present guest that I have . . . one day when I wasn't in the house, a friend came to visit her and she showed him the house, showed him her room and the friend thought the room was very nice. Then Blanca, the maid, asked them if they wanted coffee because I have always told her to be nice to them. So the maid told me that the American girl introduced her friend to her. The maid was perplexed. The girl hasn't really understood that we have them just to do the house work and that we are not friends with them.

> The maid I have now has a little baby and when the American students come, they take the child out on the street. He's one year old. It shows that they don't know how to deal with maids. I have the feeling that there in the United States they don't have different social classes. They are too friendly with the maids and end up liking the maids more than the family. One girl writes to the maid but does not have time to write to me!

> There was one girl, for example, who went against the señora and united with the maid. She would go and eat in the kitchen with the maid and said to the señora (my friend), "Why don't you let the maid eat with you?"

> They should know how to behave with the maids, not to make friends with them because they are a completely different social class. That's the problem that has happened where the students go to the maid's quarters and talk to them and the maid won't do any of the housework because she's visiting with the American girls.

In some cases the conflict generated by the interaction between the American and the maid results in the maid's quitting or being fired.

> My maid was the very talkative type. She would talk to the American girl who would come back to the house and find that the maid was the only one here. The maid would ask her different questions about life in the United States. She was not a silly maid because she had been with me for 12 years. But that is how I lost my maid. She left a week after the American girl left. She changed a lot, she was terrible! She spoke about living in the United States . . . how nice it would be. I told CEUCA that the American girl had influenced her maybe without meaning to do so, but that is why I lost my maid. The American was always nice to the maid. That was the bad part of it. I had to tell the maid not to be abusing. My daughter would tell me that the maid would get in the bedroom with the

American girl and talk. My maid got to know the American girl better than I did.

My mother had an American girl in her house who spoiled her maid completely. She would bring her up to her room and tell her things and come down to the kitchen and show the maid how to do exercises in such a way that my mother had to fire the maid.

Although most of the señoras' complaints about the guests' treatment of the maids was related to the theme of not keeping the maid at the proper social distance, other complaints were that the American was not polite and kind to the maid.

I had a lot of trouble with my second guest. She was demanding. She thought that I had 20 maids in the house and she would order the maids in a very bad way!

Sometimes Richard would get angry with the maid because she would forget something like a spoon or a knife and he would be very rude to her.

The guests should treat the maid just like my sons do. They should say "please" and "thank you" to the maids.

I had to tell my guest to be kind and well mannered with the maid when he first arrived because I had heard that they treated maids badly. I also had to say that they should not be too intimate with them.

Some of the Americans gave the impression of intending to be too intimate with the maid by addressing them with *tú* instead of the more formal *usted*. In a few cases the student had learned in a Spanish course that maids should be addressed with *tú*.

One thing I discovered that I did wrong was to use the familiar *tú* with the maid for about the first four weeks. I thought I had heard the señora use it. I had read in books that you use it with servants and people for whom you do not have a lot of respect. Then one day, some of us were talking about it and discovered that this was not the thing to have done. You should always use the polite form.

This student did not discover the error by any reaction from the maid or the señora, but from discussing it with fellow Americans who in this case happened to be correct.

Most of the host-family señoras (85 percent) said that they themselves used *usted* with their maid; the others said they always used *tú*. It is not clear why a minority takes this position. One of the señoras in explaining how she addressed her maid said that she used *tú* if the maid were very young and *usted* if she were older. Another said that she usually used *usted* because *tú* is too friendly, but that sometimes she used *tú* because "occasionally it is necessary not to seem so hard."

In any case, it would probably be permissible for the guest to use *usted* whether or not the señora did so, while it would not necessarily be correct for the guest to use *tú* even when the señora did so.

At times the señora would take emergency measures to try to break up the relationship which was "getting out of hand."

> Judy became very friendly with the maid, she would talk to her a lot and I didn't like that. . . . I didn't like for her to talk too much to the maid and ask her questions. Sometimes I would come to the house and Judy was talking to her, joking with her, so the maid wouldn't do her work. I had to tell the maid to stop laughing and get to work!

The señora would try to break up the relationship and get the maid back to work not by saying anything to the American girl but by reprimanding the maid in a way that was not understood by the American. According to the American girl the señora called downstairs to the maid and told her to stop laughing, but did not say to go to work. The American girl's reaction was:

> The maid and I get to laughing sometimes and they [the family] get upset by this. They think it is great when I laugh . . . you know, the joy of the house, the sunbeam and all that. But when Rita laughs this isn't right. She's just being silly and foolish and actually it's just the same way I am.

Thus the American girl did not realize that the señora saw the laughter as a symbol of the maid's failure to perform in the proper role and status. Several of the señoras expressed the view that it was hopeless to try to get the American to deal correctly with the maid; therefore, the only solution was what might be termed preventive isolation in which the señora became the transmitter of messages between the guest and the maid, thereby reducing social conflict by blocking direct communication.

> I don't have a live-in maid while the American guest is here. This prevents the *gringa* from getting together with the maid in her room after dinner like I hear some of them do.

> I tell Joanne not to deal with the maid directly. If she wants the maid to do something special for her, she should ask me and I'll get the maid to do it. I had to do this because Joanne would pay the maid extra and spoil her. I told her that I was already paying the maid extra while she was staying here. The maid got spoiled and started asking Joanne for more money, but I told her not to give it to her. She was happy to have me handle it for her so she would not have trouble with the maid.

> I have no trouble with the maid because I have told the guest that she should not tell anything to the maid. When she wants something done, she should ask me so that I can deal with the maid. So now she says, "Could you have Blanca do this for me?" or "Could I ask for coffee?" and that is all they say. It is better that they don't speak with the maids because they don't know how to handle them.

In host families with no children of the same age as the guest there was a stronger tendency for the *gringa* to associate with the maid who was the only person of the same sex and age as herself.

Mechanisms for enforcing the social status of the maid

From the preceding examples and other more diffused evidence we can summarize specific ways in which the social distance from the maid is maintained. We class them under the more general headings of subordination and affective neutrality.

Subordination. The maid does not eat with the family but separately in the kitchen. Only a minimum of information on the family members' personal activities, thoughts, or feelings are shared with the maid. The maid is never introduced to friends of the family she may be serving. Family members do not talk to the maid in her room but in maid's work areas. The family members generally do not address the maid with the familiar form *tú* but use *usted.* Family members do not share their clothing with the maid. Family members ordinarily do not take care of the maid's children.

Affective neutrality. The maid is neither loved like a member of the family or a friend, nor is she hated like an enemy. There are often feelings of pity or mercy toward her. Even though she is not an equal member of the family in-group she is not a dehumanized thing in the eyes of the family. She is always treated as a human being whose presence must always be acknowledged by the standard greeting phrases, and whose services must be politely requested with a "please" and acknowledged with a "thank you." While the Colombians have no difficulty maintaining the proper balance of affective neutrality, the Americans tended to vacillate between being friends with the maid or treating her as a nonentity.

The maid's functions

Some of the miscommunication and conflict generated in the inter-action between the guest and the maid was due to the American's false assumptions about the maid's functions. The American realized that specific duties come in packages according to a certain status attached to them, but the specific combination of duties constituting the maid's role in the American's mind was a North American cultural package rather than a Colombian one. This idea is clearly illustrated in the following case as seen from the conflicting points of view of the two cultures.

Mona was very ill-treated by my mother. I was amazed to find that she was only 13 years old and my mother had taken her off the street to "save her from a life of sin." She would yell at Mona to hurry up and do such and such. Like one time Mona was polishing my shoes as I had asked her in a very nice way to do because I had not brought any shoe polishing equipment with me from the States. The señora was downstairs in the kitchen and shouted at the maid who was in her

151

own room polishing my shoes, "What are you doing? You are supposed to be preparing dinner. It is already 7:45 and you haven't started!" She is always putting on the pressure to do more and faster and criticizing this little girl.

Ronald, my current American student, is a wonderful person in general. He is like a lot of the *norteamericanos* because he was very familiar with the maid. He treated her like his little sister. But then he started feeling sorry for her for a while, then later he began to get angry with her. For example, after he had been here about two months he started making her polish his shoes and making her do extra work for him which is not the kind of thing a maid should do.

The American did not realize that polishing shoes was not considered a function of the maid and that, even though he had not brought any shoe polishing equipment with him, he could either have bought it in Bogotá or had the shoeshine boy polish his shoes for one peso.

There was also a clear tendency for the American to assume that, since there was a maid or possibly two, there would be a lot of *extra* services available for all the family members. He unconsciously assumed that, since his family in the United States had no domestic help, the maids were to provide *extra* services. What he had forgotten is that the *bogotano* home is much less mechanized and much of the daily household routine is more time consuming because of the lack of electrical appliances like automatic washing machines, electric toasters, clothes dryers, hair dryers, food freezers, vacuum cleaners, and automatic ovens.

Just as important for labor saving are the partially prepared foods such as frozen or canned vegetables and fruits, frozen orange juice which does not have to be squeezed from the fruit, and bread which is already cut. Canned fruits are much too expensive for everyday use so raw ones must be selected, peeled, and cooked. Since there are fewer prepared foods, the groceries tend to be more bulky. If the family does not have a car the maid has to make many more trips to the market per week than would be needed in the United States. Also, there are fewer supermarkets where all of the food can be purchased in the same place; so buying food involves many more stops.

These and many other details make it more difficult to perform the basic functions of cooking, washing dishes, washing clothes, and shopping in Bogotá than in middle-class United States. Therefore, the presence of a maid does not actually represent extra service. There is still considerable work left for the señora to do, especially if there are children.

The American also tends to overestimate the actual amount of help the maid provides if he thinks of the maid as being a housekeeper in the same sense as his own mother in the States. There is a vast difference mainly because of the different educational level. Many maids neither read nor write. Most have less than a third grade education. The range of tasks which they can do is much smaller, the flexibility with which they can coordinate and reschedule activities is much less, they are slower to learn a new task, their ability to control the children is much less, and the maids' tendency to make costly errors when working with any kind of appliances is much greater. To the American it seems clear that the *bogotano* household has a simpler, more predictable and less diversified pattern of activities than his home in the United States. Part of the source of this simplicity and predictability is due to the necessity of adjusting to the limitations of the maid in combination with the absence of many household labor saving devices.

The señoras sometimes recognized the American's tendency to expect too much of the maids.

> Yes, I had a lot of problems. The Americans are amazed when they find maids here. They say that in the United States only rich people have maids. So they think we are rich too and that they are going to live like a guest in a rich home, but they are disappointed.

> The Americans were surprised to see how we live . . . with maids and everything. It surprises them and they think that it is a luxury and that we are millionaires, but later they understand that all of us have maids, even humble families. But the American thinks that this means there is nothing for him to do in the house.

> These American girls take advantage of the fact that there are maids here and they won't do a lot of things they ordinarily do in the United States.

> She must have thought I had a dozen maids the way she ordered them to do this and to do that. She would ring the buzzer in her room in the morning and ask the maid to bring her coffee or fruit juice. Also, she gave all of her underclothes to the maid to wash. I wash my own underclothes and she should too.

There were also those Americans who noticed that the maid had plenty of work so would try to help in some way. But without a clear knowledge of the maid's duties their attempts to help could lead to a different type of conflict.

> Sometimes it is obvious that help is needed with the meals, but the *muchacha* (maid) gets mad if I pitch in and set the table.

> I tried to help the maid with the washing but it was obvious that she was embarrassed.

> When I swept out my room, the señora came rushing in and said "No, no! Let Obdulia do that."

And from the señoras:

> John was the one who used to go into the kitchen and fiddle around. The maid complained to me and I had to tell him not to do anything in the kitchen.

One of the girls used to try to help the maid with the breakfast dishes. I didn't know that because I usually left the house before she did. Then the maid told me that the American girl must not be satisfied with the way she did the dishes, so I told the girl. Everything has been all right since then.

But there are acceptable ways to help.

I have always had good maids so there isn't anything for the *gringas* to do. Of course when I have people invited for dinner and I get in the kitchen, they ask me if I want them to help me, and I say, "Of course," because my own daughters do that too.

Much of the time I did not have a maid, so I would do everything and the *gringa* would cooperate. Then when I took a maid she didn't like it because she felt more comfortable without a maid and said she could help me instead. So when this maid quit I didn't hire another one while Betty was here.

It is easy for the Colombian host to draw false conclusions that the guest is lazy, inconsiderate, or arrogant when this is not the case. The American with the best of intentions can be judged lazy for failing to do certain things, such as making the bed, which he falsely assumes to be the maid's duty. At the same time he can be judged negatively for trying to help in a wrong way which tends to usurp the maid's duties or to irritate the señora by "spoiling the maid." Most of the American guests seemed to learn more quickly what they were not supposed to do because it was the maid's duty, than they were to learn what they were supposed to do because it was not the maid's duty.

I would give my eye teeth for a nice big juicy rare hamburger and I'd love to have a kitchen where I could cook myself, because I just love to cook. And my mother knows that I love to cook, but she doesn't worry about it because she also knows that I'm not going to cook when I'm here unless she invites me to do it at a time when it will not interfere with the maid. I think that Mercedes (the maid) would be very insulted. So I wouldn't do it. She is too sweet.

This is typical; practically all of the *gringas* soon realized that the kitchen was off limits for them unless it was some special occasion in which the señora had invited them to work and was usually working with them; yet a sizable proportion of the American guests did not realize that their señora expected them to make their own bed. This contrast is probably not due to the American's reluctance to be active so much as it is a manifestation of the principle that one's sins of commission are more likely to be corrected than his sins of omission.

One of the basic functions of the maid which the North American guests sometimes failed to appreciate was what might be called her "house sitting" function. In some cases the guests thought of the señora as a social butterfly who could leave all the household work to the maid and go out to visit friends, window shop, or pursue any sort of leisure-time activity. Most of the señoras did not go out in the morning because that was when the maid was most likely to run errands while the señora did certain household chores of her own, and it was necessary that the maid or some adult member of the family be in the house at all times. Not only is there the possibility of theft, but also it is necessary to have a person who can receive deliveries.

Legal protections for the maid

The majority of the American guests had very little objective knowledge about the maid in their Colombian home. For example, 76 percent said they did not know the maid's salary and the other 24 percent either greatly underestimated or overestimated the maid's pay. Although only 37 percent of the guests admitted that they did not know the amount of time off the maid had, estimates of another 40 percent were obviously assumptions untested by actual observation. Actually, both the amount of pay and time off is fairly standard for the live-in maid. According to law, the live-in maid must have off every other Sunday and an additional half-day each week. The maid's compensation consists of her board and room, a salary of from 200 to 400 pesos ($12 to $25) per month; also a uniform and shoes are furnished periodically. She must be given one month's notice if she is fired after a two-week trial period, and she receives a paid vacation each year. She is also entitled to certain medical and maternity costs.

Under this system the señoras seemed to worry sometimes about their live-in maid becoming pregnant. Some mentioned that they thought they should get rid of their maid who had been "seeing too much of the young policeman on the beat." To the American guests it was a mystery where the maid and her boyfriend might meet to have any privacy; the house was strictly off limits for any boyfriend and the maid usually came back before dark (6:30 p.m.) on her days off. Nevertheless, it was clear that this was a source of worry for some of the señoras.

Frequently, the American guest would draw conclusions regarding the señora's character and her motivations because he thought the particular señora in his home was particularly demanding in the amount of hours the maid worked and uniquely ungenerous in the amount she paid the maid. Often the North American simply substituted his assumptions for the facts and had little appreciation of the problem from the señora's point of view. The point here is that both the maid and the señora are performing in accord with a clear paternalistic pattern that has been partially written into the labor code, rather than in terms of their individual personality traits.

One type of response from the American guests is to feel sorry for the maid and to give or loan her money. It was interesting to note that, in spite of the fact that many of the guests felt sorry for the maid, most of them said that they would like to have a maid if they lived in Bogotá. Some felt that they could offer the maid a much more pleasant working situation than their Colombian host.

Of course none of these young Americans had the opportunity to hire a maid, but the impression given by the American families in Bogotá is that they are disappointed in their efforts to "democratize" or to Americanize the maid, and they are divided on the issue of whether home life is better for the wife in Bogotá with a maid or in the United States without one. Actually, this is an idle comparison since the household tasks are very different in the two situations.

In view of the American guests' lack of experience not only with maids but also with running a household, it is not surprising that considerable misunderstanding could be centered around the maid. The guest and the host both made uncomplimentary judgments about the other as a result of the American's lack of understanding of the maid's role and function in the household. If the American thought his host treated the maid incorrectly, it was usually in terms of "mistreating" her in some way. If the host had a complaint about the American guest's treatment of the maid it was usually in terms of either "spoiling" the maid or "ignoring" her by not extending the common courtesy of greetings. One thing that emerged clearly from all of the accounts of the guest's dealings with the maid was that it was virtually impossible to get along well with the señora if one did not get along with the maid. The maid was clearly an extension of the señora's ego.

Relationships with Others

Children

If the children were young (up to 12 years), there were complaints from the American guest that they did not respect his privacy, that they carefully inspected the contents of his drawers and bedroom closet. Some families seemed to assume that this was perfectly natural and that any door or drawer that was not locked was open for inspection. The American guest had difficulty in knowing how to strike the appropriate balance between being victimized by the young child's demands and over-reacting to what he feels to be the inconsiderate behavior "of a spoiled brat."

The American guests felt that the young boys in the family were more spoiled than the girls. This is particularly interesting in view of the fact

156

that several of the señoras expressed the belief that American children were spoiled by indulgent parents who treated them like equals.

What is probably operating here is the clash between the two sets of cultural assumptions regarding the proper pattern of rights, duties, and privileges to be accorded to children by the adults. In observing the behavior of children in the other culture, each person tends to notice those behaviors that are taboo in his own culture but tolerated in the other culture. This toleration appears as overindulgence to the person whose culture does not permit a certain behavior. Thus, each thinks the other culture's children are "spoiled."

It is much more difficult to note the special responsibilities or prohibitions assumed by the child in the other culture. For example, many Colombian parents and teachers thought of the new programmed learning type of workbooks used in United States schools as just another indication of the American adults "catering to the spoiled brats who are too lazy to copy a paragraph from the board, copy the 10 questions about the paragraph, and then write out the answers and memorize them." They missed the point that, by saving the student this much time spent in exercising his hand muscles, he was expected to internalize certain *thought* processes that would provide a deeper, more flexible, and creative understanding of the problem. In a few cases, the American guest got so irritated with the Colombian child that he "decided to act like a real member of the family and give the kid a good spanking." According to the Americans who tried this tactic it "got marvelous results." According to the señoras it was a debatable way of acting like a member of the family.

In the host families with college-aged children (who lived at home), the guest–child relationship brought different kinds of communication problems. For example, there were misunderstandings regarding whether or not the *colombiana* had gotten permission to wear certain of the *gringa's* dresses and vice versa. There was the problem of the *gringa* falling in love with the son in the family. This became a serious problem in a few cases. In one case the señora requested that the *gringa* be transferred to another family. In another case the señora blamed the *gringa* for the fact that her son had failed the whole year's work in college. However, this situation was usually avoided because families with college-aged sons did not often take a girl but insisted on a boy. There was even greater care not to have an American boy in a family with a Colombian daughter of college age.

Another problem was found in the American's attempt to use the Colombian son or daughter as a dating bureau, tourist guide, and errand boy. The American often expected this family with a college-aged child to be an ideal setup. The American guest would often ask the "fellow student" for types of favors he would not dare ask of the parents in the household. In a few cases there was a tendency for the American to try to monopolize the Colombian's time in the kinds of activities he preferred, or felt capable of participating in, or felt he needed the help of the Colombian to participate in. For the American to expect to have a temporary monopoly on the Colombian's free time assumes either that the Colombian did not have any other friends or social activities before the American arrived or that he should gladly forsake them for the duration of the American guest's stay. This was particularly a problem in the many cases where the American preferred to be with just the one Colombian rather than share with his Colombian friends in some activity of the Colombians' choosing. This was accentuated, of course, by the added fact that some of the Colombians preferred to be with the American alone because they felt that the American did not get along well in the group activities or would be a bore to their friends.

Another general problem was that the American guest often unwittingly acted as a wedge between the parents and the children. Sometimes the initiative in driving the wedge was taken by the American and sometimes by the Colombian. At times the American set an example of greater freedom and independence than had been accorded to the Colombian child by his parents. This might be in the area of dating, staying out at night, wearing mini-skirts, slacks, or shorts, not making his bed, etc.

The American was sometimes an unwitting victim of the Colombian son's or daughter's attempt to use him to obtain certain concessions from the parents. For example, one daughter persuaded the *gringa* to tell the father that she would like to go horseback riding which the father had never let the daughter do. The father would give in to the guest's request and could no longer refuse his own daughter who naturally went along. In another case, the son would have the American boy say that they had been out together in the evening when in fact the Colombian boy was secretly with his girl friend. In two instances the Colombian señora was considerably irritated because her son always spoke English, which she could not understand, with the American boy in front of her. She felt that her son was hiding something from her. Rightly in this case; he was usually plotting to get the American's cooperation in evading the supervision of his parents.

The father

There is little evidence of communication problems between the guest and the father in the Colombian family because there was a minimum of father–guest interaction. The señor spent relatively little time at home, and these times were usually the times when the American was least likely to be there himself. For example, the father had lunch at home more frequently than dinner, but the American was much more likely to eat lunch in town or on campus than he was to eat dinner out.

The guests were reluctant to take up any of the father's time when he seemed to have so little time at home with the family. The father often did not arrive home until 7:30 p.m., would have dinner and go immediately to the master bedroom upstairs. The father's main time with his wife and children was on weekends which began after lunch Saturdays since many men work on Saturday mornings. On Sunday the family might choose to go to an early mass in order to have time for a picnic or movie or some other family outing. Unless the guest went on this family outing, he would not see much of the señor that week.

Another quite different reason for few reports of interaction with the señor was that approximately a third of the host families had no father present either because he had died or the couple had separated. In other cases the father worked out of Bogotá and would commute once or twice a month to see the family.

When the señora was asked about how the guest got along with the father, the reply was usually very positive. There were some reports that the señor did not like the idea of a stranger living in the house. He thought it would infringe upon the family's privacy or would force him to treat the guest formally. Usually these initial reservations were overcome by the señora's suggestion that they try it for a short time. This attitude was also encouraged by some of the American sponsoring organizations. In most cases the señor's reservations dissolved.

Some of the señoras did report that the guest did not get along well with the señor because the American had acted as a wedge between him and the children. Another facet of the guest–father communication was the miscommunication generated in their discussions of current events, international affairs, coffee prices, United States–Latin American relations.

Neighbors and friends

There were instances when visiting neighbors, friends, or relatives felt that the American guest was unfriendly because, when they were introduced, the American would excuse himself as quickly as possible to go to his room. Often this was because the American did not realize that the visitors had come specifically to meet him, yet this had not been stated by the host. In other cases it was simply that the family expected the guest to act like a member of the family in socializing with their friends.

Also, the Americans were less likely than the Colombians to perceive anyone five or ten years older or two years younger as appropriate for them to socialize with. The age range of the Colombians attending a house party was much greater than that in the parties the guest had been accustomed to in the United States.

Another type of miscommunication between the guest and the neighbors was often achieved without the exchange of a single word. In these cases some action by the guest caused repercussions often unknown to the guest but clearly reported to the señora by her neighbors. For example, in several cases the señora reported that the *gringa* was seen kissing some boy goodnight on the front doorstep. Even more serious were those cases where the señora was a widow and the neighbors might assume that it was the señora herself on the front doorstep at 2:00 a.m. rather than the *gringa*. In one such case the neighbors did not report the event to the señora. When she discovered it for herself, she had to announce the discovery to the neighbors and friends to protect her own reputation. In this case the señora's attempt to advise the *gringa* failed because the señora did not directly say that she was worried about her own reputation, but put it in terms of the girl's reputation. The girl's reaction was that the señora should not be such a busy-body and worry about her reputation since she, herself, was not worried.

In other cases the señora felt repercussions from the neighbors when the *gringa* took sunbaths in her bikini in the back patio. In another case, the *gringa* was doing exercises on the front lawn while dressed in shorts. The exercises being done in that location would be worth some comment even without the added attraction of the shorts.

In these cases there are communication problems because the señora wants to correct the girl's behavior, but she is not sure it is worth the effort. She finds it difficult to believe the *gringa* does not know that this is unusual behavior. Also, the *gringa* finds it difficult to believe that the señora is not exaggerating the reaction of the neighbors and tends to attribute some dark motives to the señora.

Notes

1. We should not forget that there are many acceptable ways for the male guest to pull his part of the load in the home such as making his bed well, keeping his room neat, hanging his towel out to dry.
2. These tasks are arranged in rank order according to their relative importance in the eyes of the Colombians, with the task that is most important for the guest to help with at the top of the list.

9

Implications for Foreign Language Teachers and Cross-Cultural Trainers

This description, analysis and interpretation of the communication barriers between North Americans and their Colombian host families has an obvious practical orientation value for those who expect to live with a Latin American family abroad. In addition it has a more general value to those who would like a better understanding of how the cross-culturally dissonant silent assumptions act as barriers to communication for anyone immersed in any foreign culture.

Practical Orientational Value

The reader cannot expect to find a precise description of any specific *bogotano* family with whom he has lived or may live in the future. Colombian family patterns vary according to the region from which a particular family comes and its socioeconomic class, and there is a general historical change in the family patterns for Colombia and all of Latin America. Many of the differences we found in family living patterns were associated with these three major dimensions of culture variation.

Family-living patterns also varied with the phase of the family life cycle, with differences in education, with the degree of international experience and with other background variables. Many of the host families involved in this study came from outside of Bogotá and the state of Cundinamarca. They included a full range of the family life cycle from those with only pre-school children to widows whose children are grown and married. There was a wide variation in international experience: Some had received the secondary and college education abroad; others had never been outside of Colombia. In view of these wide variations in background, it is remarkable that we found as many similarities among the families as we did.

Not only was there considerable variation in the backgrounds of the hosts, but also of the American guests. They came from all regions of the United States except the Deep South. They had attended widely different kinds of colleges and universities: large and small, private and state, religious and secular. Their religious backgrounds included mainly Baptist, Catholic, Mennonite, Methodist, Presbyterian, Quaker and Unitarian. The American guests were mainly middle class and were between the ages of 19 and 26. All of those 24 years or older were Peace Corps trainees.

The variation in the types of American guests and in the host families served to emphasize the more general differences between the North American and Colombian cultures. We were impressed by the fact that it was precisely those characteristics shared by the *bogotano* host families that were most likely to differ from those shared by the Americans.

Despite the existence of a pattern of behavior among the host families, there are varying proportions of exceptions depending upon which cultural trait we are describing. For example, we saw that there was more agreement among the host families that the guest should take a bath at least once a day than on whether the guest should address the host with the polite *usted* or the familiar *tú* form.[1]

Although not all of the culture patterns are uniformly followed by all of the host families, this information on the modes and the relative amount of deviation from the modal patterns has a practical value in becoming oriented to the *bogotano* middle-class family. It alerts us to the fact that there is the possibility of a different pattern of behavior not found in the United States. For example, the hand-to-forearm greeting used among Colombian women may not be used in a given situation, but if it is used, it will be used only between women. With this much advance information, we are not caught by surprise, and we are sensitized to the need to sharpen our observation so that we can imitate or discover the criteria to determine the appropriate occasion for its use. Even a partial knowledge of the criteria of appropriateness of the behavior is better than none.

The real danger in this kind of incomplete knowledge lies in two types of misuse. The first is the failure to distinguish between the simple existence versus the acceptability of a certain overt behavior pattern. The person who is trying to learn through direct observation of the foreign behavior patterns runs the danger of assuming that any behavior pattern of the natives would be acceptable for him to imitate. Thus, an American girl might note that Colombian girls walk unaccompanied in the downtown streets after 11:00 p.m., so she is surprised that her Colombian host objects to this behavior. The American girl feels that this act does not violate the cultural norms because she observed it done by Colombian girls her own age. The problem here is that the Colombian girl she is using as her model is probably a prostitute. The Colombian host is concerned not only with the American girl's reputation but with her own reputation because people might think that she has a prostitute for a house guest. This type of error is most likely to occur when the behavior pattern witnessed either is one that does occur and is acceptable in the North American culture or is a behavior pattern perceived as a "new freedom" by the foreigner.

The second error is to assume that if a certain behavior pattern is obviously not considered deviant or immoral, it is appropriate for all. For example, in some *bogotano* households it was considered a privilege of only the señora to have breakfast in bed; in others this was also extended to the señor; in others to daughters but not to sons. When a custom varies from family to family, the problem is to discover which family members are considered eligible to participate in the pattern in any particular household. In one home where it was customary for the teenage daughters to have breakfast in bed, a *gringa* guest incorrectly inferred that she was not being treated like a member of the family but like a special guest when the maid brought coffee and orange juice to her room each morning. In another household the señora thought that the *gringa* was demanding special services because she buzzed to have the maid bring up her coffee, while the *gringa* simply felt that she was imitating the señora's behavior. This type of problem often occurs in situations where the North American "democratically" assumes that we all have equal rights, privileges, and duties.

We can use the information about *bogotano* families creatively as a guide to our own behavior, even though some parts of the behavior patterns are not followed by all families and even though we are not given complete information on the criteria that determine who can follow the pattern under what conditions.

In addition to having some practical value for those who will be living with a Latin American family, this description of the communication problems of the American guest in the Colombian home will have value for anyone interested in understanding the general problem of cross-cultural communication or in discovering the specific nonlinguistic barriers in a totally different cultural setting. This more general purpose will be served insofar as we have been able to illustrate certain tentative generalizations about the basic nature of cross-cultural communication.

Some Tentative Generalizations

We feel that the value of this study goes beyond the discovery and description of specific culture patterns that acted as barriers to communication between American guests and their Colombian hosts, to a more general understanding of the nature of cross-cultural communication as it is affected by the dissonant silent assumptions. Let us now summarize some of the tentative generalizations that are in harmony with the data we have presented here with data presented in other monographs based on this project,[2] and with other data and insights gained in the process of doing this field study.

Syllogistic nature of meaning

There are certain covert assumptions which act as the context for interpreting the meaning of the overt message. Thus, the silent assumption is the major premise, the message is the minor premise and the meaning is the conclusion of the syllogism. In a sense the message is the raw material for interpretation by the listener. His interpretation depends upon the *silent assumptions* that remain unexpressed either because they are unconscious or because the communicators assume them to be self-evident and universally understood and, therefore, not needing to be expressed. They are taken for granted in the situation where the dialogue takes place.

Situation-associated assumptions

The particular assumptions that are applied in interpreting the message are linked with the situation itself *not* with the words, gestures or tone of voice used in the message. This point is vital to the understanding of cross-cultural communication. This means that the correct translation in the purely linguistic sense is not enough to assure successful communication. If the American were not speaking Spanish but had an interpreter who would always make a perfect translation for him, this would not eliminate the communication barrier we have been investigating. Furthermore, we cannot assure communication by establishing the "true meaning" of the words in Spanish or English by comparing, for example, the words (images or feelings) associated in the Colombian's mind with the word *familia* with those associated in the American's mind with the word *family*.[3] This approach would reveal some interesting cultural differences, but it would not reflect the different silent contexts used to interpret any statements about the family or statements made in the context of interaction with the Colombian family.

This fact that the relevant assumptions are associated with the situation has very valuable practical implications for anyone wanting to learn the sociocultural context needed to communicate in a foreign country. He need not learn all of the patterns of the foreign culture, but can begin with patterns that are relevant to the particular situations in which he will be required to operate. Here the concept of "situation" includes the *objectives* of the interaction, the *time* and *space* patterns of the *activities* involved, the *roles* (functions, division of labor and status) of the actors in the situation and the *rules* (norms, values, ideals, regulations and laws) governing the interaction in that situation. These can be learned situation by situation. The task is further limited to knowing how to perform only one particular role in that situation. Thus, what is needed by the American guest to participate successfully in and communicate about the *bogotano* household is quite different from the knowledge needed to work as an auto mechanic in Bogotá.

Of course there are elements in one situation which are equivalent to elements in another. For example, an understanding of the Spanish personal naming system may be needed in a variety of situations such as introducing a friend, using a library, making a telephone call, obtaining an identification card, or watching a play. In contrast, knowing the rules of a *tejo* game[4] would be useful only in playing, watching, or talking about the game.

The relevant silent assumptions constituting the major premise can be an abstract philosophical idea or a concrete "rule of the game." The level of abstraction in the major premise depends upon the nature of the situation and the level of abstraction of the messages exchanged in that situation. Thus, if a conversation revolves around arriving at some agreement on intellectual concepts, the meaning will be interpreted in terms of highly abstract assumptions. Conversely, if the conversation revolves around coordinating an activity (eating dinner, inviting someone, sharing expenses, getting a bath) the relevant silent assumptions needed to interpret the conversation are such things as when and where these activities are supposed to take place, who does what in each situation, and how the particular physical props are to be used in pursuing each activity. Once we understand all of these dimensions of the situation, conversations about these situations become more meaningful.

Cross-culturally dissonant assumptions

The guest trying to communicate in the foreign culture automatically applies the assumptions from his own culture to the situation in which he is interacting unless he understands and has learned to respond in terms of the foreign assumptions. When the external cues to the situation in the foreign country are more similar to those of the guest's culture, he is less likely to question the applicability of his own assumptions or wonder about the rules that might apply in the foreign setting. For example, the banks in Bogotá look familiar to the North American, so he assumes that cashing a check in pesos at the Banco de Bogotá is the same procedure as cashing a dollar check at the First National Bank in Miami. When he begins to have difficulty in the bank and people's conversation ceases to make sense, he may still not question his assumptions about how to cash a check because they are mainly unconscious.

In contrast, he immediately suspects that he will have difficulty in situations for which there is no United States equivalent, as in buying a national lottery ticket, attending a bullfight, playing *tejo* or a game of chance called *cinco y seis*.

To illustrate further, the North American Protestant is not surprised that he has some difficulty learning how to behave at mass in Bogotá, but often the North American Catholic has a distinct shock in store for him when he attends mass because he discovers that the interaction in the church is quite different from that he has been accustomed to in the United States.

Values, conflict, and communication

Differences in cultural values as such were rarely a cause of mis-communication in the situations studied here. We tend to think that the really important differences between cultures are the differences in values. This may or may not be true, but it seems to be clearly an error to assume that value dissonances constitute the silent assumptions that cause mis-communication. We did not find any evidence to support this contention. Instead, we noted that often conflict can be brought about through communication. This happens when two people discover that their cherished values are in conflict.

166

Conflict is also brought about between people with the same values in situations where there is a shortage of valued objects and the two parties are in competition for the same thing. This conflict or competition is not due to miscommunication.

We have also cited cases where the two parties in a cross-cultural situation have precisely the same basic goals in a particular interaction situation, yet there is considerable miscommunication because of the dissonant assumptions about the means (time, place, division of labor, sequences of actions, etc.) by which the goals are to be achieved. This was seen in the communication failure between host and guest regarding the bathing situation when both cultures placed a high value upon bodily cleanliness and bathing. The confusion was in the differences between how this end was to be achieved. We also discovered situations in which miscommunication led one person to perceive the other as having different values when in fact he did not.

There is one sense, however, in which value differences can cause miscommunication. When each of the communicating parties feels strongly about his own values which are in opposition to the other's values, this dissonance may raise emotions to such a level that each party is unable to draw logical conclusions from the same major and minor premises. Just because they have a value conflict in relationship to one issue does not mean that they would also logically disagree on other issues, yet the emotion of distrust and hostility may cause miscommunication on the issues where there is no disagreement in the major premises.

Trivial misunderstandings have profound effects

Sometimes people interested in cross-cultural understanding assume that we should not waste our time trying to understand the "trivial" cultural patterns of daily living, but should plumb the depths of the profound philosophical underpinnings of the culture or probe the psychoanalytic labyrinth of the national character. This study shows that it is precisely in these "trivial" problems of coping with the activities of daily living that misunderstandings accumulate causing the participants to make profound judgments of each other's character. This is probably most true of situations where there is daily cross-cultural contact.

We showed how the American guests' false assumptions about mealtime, bathtime, use of hot water, locking doors, location of the television set, and many other mundane details making up the cultural pattern of the *bogotano* household, led to serious miscalculations by the host families regarding the guests' character.

There were two distinctly different ways in which the "trivial" misunderstandings led to basic judgments. First, there was the direct mis-interpretation of the American's intent or motivation. For example, the guest might refrain from making his bed not because he is thoughtless but because he falsely assumes that this is the maid's duty. Second is the indirect route in which the miscommunication causes the American to act in a way he himself does not approve. He acts this way either because he feels incorrectly that he is doing as the natives do or because he cannot solve the communication problems involved in the attempt to behave according to his own standards. In the case of bathing the American's standard was the same as the Colombian's. The judgment of some Colombians that Americans "sometimes smell bad" was true, but it was not a result of the Americans' desire to be dirty.

Making allowances for foreigners

Sometimes the Americans who discover that the Colombians have been making negative judgments of their behavior or character are angered by the "intolerance" of the Colombian. Sometimes they express their reaction in rhetorical questions such as, "Don't they make any allowances for the fact that I am a foreigner?" "Do they expect me to be a Colombian just because I crossed the border?" "Since I make allowances for them, why can't they make allowances for me?"

Although these questions are usually rhetorical, there are some answers we discovered and clarified in the process of doing this research. First, the Colombians did make allowances for the fact that their guest was a foreigner. For example, several hosts reported making special efforts to speak clearly, omit colloquialisms, and slow down the pace. Also, many reported giving the *gringas* freedoms not allowed to their own daughters. Further, they attempted to give explanations and advice which was not needed by their own children at the same age. They forgave errors of all kinds when they realized they were unintentional. They even protected the American's ego by not telling him that he had made certain social errors.

Then is the American guest totally wrong in feeling that the Colombians did *not* make allowances for him? No, he is correct to a certain extent. The basic problem is that the Colombian could make allowances for certain behavior only if he realized that the reason was actually the guest's foreign status. The crucial point here is that, if the American behaves in a way completely strange and exotic to the Colombian, then he realizes that this is a foreign custom whether he likes it or not. However, if the Americans behave in a way which is familiar but disapproved by the Colombian, he will perceive this as evidence of the Americans' undesirable character. It is an act performed only by bad Colombians.

Much of the American's communication difficulty is in his inability (rather than his unwillingness) to make allowances for his own foreign status. He does not know what it is that he does not know in order to understand what is going on about him. The Colombian is unable to distinguish in many situations between the American's inability and his unwillingness to conform to the behavior norms of a given situation.

The American who speaks Spanish with a heavy accent will have more allowances made for him than the American who speaks Spanish fluently. The Colombians seemed to assume that anyone who speaks Spanish fluently with no accent also knows the other culture patterns, therefore any violation of these patterns is intentional.

Vicious circle effect

There is a tendency for minor communication breakdowns to lead to further breakdowns of communication in the following way. Misunderstandings over small, everyday activities led the Colombians to make judgments about the American's desires and motivations and about how other Colombians would react to him. These judgments, right or wrong, have the effect of opening or closing the doors to participation in various social situations.

When trivial misunderstandings lead to strong negative images of the American, this in turn leads to social isolation of the American, which leads to noncommunication; and this makes it more difficult for the American to discover the Colombians' silent assumptions he needs to know to communicate with them. Thus the circle is complete, and the American becomes a prisoner of isolation. Somehow this vicious circle must be broken if we are to communicate successfully on more than a superficial level with members of any foreign culture.

The danger of the blind leading the blind

The findings in this study have important implications for many orientation programs in which American returnees from abroad are used to instruct and orient other Americans about to go abroad to the same country. This system is used to some extent by the Peace Corps, by foreign study programs sponsored by colleges, by business firms sending staff abroad, by the United States Army and other government agencies. The important question is, "Do the accounts of an amateur observer regarding any foreign culture provide objective information or simply ethnocentric distortions of reality produced by systematic misinterpretation of cross-cultural experience?"

Insofar as ethnocentric distortions predominate in the observer's report, this system of orientation will simply compound the error. It will crystallize as sacred truth certain misinterpretations. Insofar as this distortion of communication exists, we would expect the "observations" reported by the American, the Spaniard, the German, the Russian, or the Japanese to be clearly different on certain points even though they are reporting on the same culture.

For example, Peace Corps trainees told other trainees that Colombians were very rude in their behavior in a bank, because they would butt in at the head of the line. Actually, there was no line and there should not have been a line. The Colombians were saying that the Americans were rude because they were violating the rules for cashing checks. Also, American students studying in Bogotá would tell others that the taxi drivers are not to be trusted because they cheat by collecting more than the amount on the meter. They sometimes explained that señoras in the host families are lazy and selfish, that the Colombian fathers do not love their children, that the host families do not expect them to bathe more than twice a week, that the American guest is expected to take a cold shower, that it is permissible to go barefooted anywhere in the house, that it is permissible to wear shorts to a picnic, that the registration system at the universities is very disorganized, and that you should not make your own bed but leave it for the maid. These and many other bits of practical advice are given in total sincerity but in each case the advice was usually based upon misinterpretation of their observations.

Are we then doomed to say that all observations by Americans abroad are distorted and useless for orienting others to go abroad? I suggest some criteria of the probable validity of information given by Americans returning from abroad:

1. If the reporter is able to separate his actual observations from his interpretation and conclusions drawn from the observations, his information is more useful and valid.
2. If it is possible to separate the *concrete* facts from the *abstract* generalization in the information reported, the information becomes more useful.
3. Information reported on the more objective situation is generally more reliable than reports on the foreigner's subjective state.
4. Information that the foreign culture is just like the United States or that United States patterns of behavior are acceptable should be subjected to close scrutiny.

This whole research project was based on the assumption that the safest way to avoid the problem of the blind leading the blind was to adopt a field strategy in which the interaction between Americans and Colombians was studied by a cross-cultural team of Americans and Colombians. The Americans were interviewed by Americans regarding their interaction with Colombians and the Colombians were interviewed by Colombians regarding their interaction with these same Americans. In this way we avoided having to make any of the following questionable assumptions:

1. That the Americans were aware of when they were miscommunicating.
2. That Americans knew what the nature of the communication problem was.
3. That Americans had discovered how to avoid specific communication problems.
4. That Colombians are willing to tell Americans the negative images they have of them.
5. That Colombians' conclusions regarding the Americans' intentions are correct.
6. That either Colombians or Americans are capable of distinguishing between their raw observations and their interpretation of them.
7. That either Americans or Colombians are aware of how the same message would be interpreted differently by Americans and Colombians.

This is not the place to give a detailed treatment of the methodological problems and solutions in such a cross-cultural study. However, we discovered that the use of a bilingual and bicultural team was the most basic characteristic of the methodology which allowed us to efficiently and validly gain access to the barriers to communication we were trying to discover. Essentially, we had to find a way to avoid getting bogged down in the same cross-cultural miscommunication we were attempting to study.

Fortuitous Factors in the Encounter

Why do some North Americans encounter difficulties in operating in a given situation while others do not? Sometimes the answer is simply that some have discovered the cultural pattern and others have not, but it was not always this simple. We found that some Americans who did *not* understand the pattern were having no difficulties. They often thought they understood the pattern since they had not been experiencing any personal inconvenience, not realizing that their success was due to one of several fortuitous factors. Here the word "fortuitous" is used to refer to those factors other than the differences between the Colombian and American assumptions governing the situation. The differences between the two culture patterns determine the types of misunderstandings that could *potentially* occur in a given cross-cultural situation. Whether or not a particular one of these misunderstandings actually arises depends upon one or more of the following:[5]

1. *Which of the patterns of action from the guest's own culture he attempts to follow in the host culture.* For example, in the guest's own culture it is permissible to bathe in hot water any time of the day or night with no special arrangements. But if his personal preference is to bathe in the morning, he would encounter a different set of communication barriers from those he would meet if he tried to bathe at night.

2. *Which particular bit of information (based on either observation or conversation) the guest happens to receive first.* For example, a host may decide to explain to the guest that it is perfectly permissible to bathe in the evening *if* he asks the maid to turn on the heater and *if* he will turn it off when his bath is finished. On the other hand, information may be misinterpreted to activate a barrier. For example, if he happened to observe that the maid washes the dinner dishes in cold water without any explanation from the *señora* he would conclude that he should not take a hot bath at night.

3. *Which cultural pattern is being followed by the members of the host family.* In some families, for example, the señora eats breakfast in her room after her husband leaves for work at 7:30, then takes her morning bath at 8:00. In other families, the husband and wife eat together after both have bathed. In this case there would be no conflict with the guest who bathes at 7:30 to get to his 8:30 class.

4. *Which of several possible physical arrangements exist in a particular household.* The number of bathrooms upstairs in the host's home could vary from one to three. If there are three, at least one of these is attached to the parents' master bedroom. If there are two used by the children and there are two or more children of each sex, it is common for one of the bathrooms to be used by males and the other by females.

Learning the pattern

Many stumbling blocks deter the guest from learning the relevant patterns of the host culture. The visitor may assume that the host family will tell him what the pattern is. However, this is expecting too much cross-cultural knowledge on the part of the host, who usually has no idea what the foreign guest does not know. Once the guest begins to recognize this, he might expect the host to tell him when he makes mistakes in his attempt to adjust to the household activities.

Middle-class *bogotanos* are brought up according to Spanish cultural patterns; their speech, especially regarding polite forms, is often indirect. On the contrary, the North American speaks very directly and concretely. The Colombian host assumes that his American guest has not been brought up properly (*mal educado*) and would not be open to suggestion. The host might also be inhibited by considerations of etiquette toward a foreign guest.

The host might try to advise the guest, but he is unsuccessful. Sometimes the guest does not realize that he is receiving advice, or sometimes the host cannot explain the situation in terms the guest can understand. Sometimes the guest chooses not to follow the advice given.

The guest who does not expect the host to take the initiative feels quite justified in assuming that if he asks the host for advice, the host should and could supply the needed advice. This assumption is sometimes realistic; in other cases it is not depending upon the nature of the problem about which he asks for advice, whether he does convey to the host that he is sincerely asking for advice, and how the guest has reacted to any previous advice he has received from the host.

When the American guest begins to discover some of the barriers to learning from his host, he may begin to rely more and more upon his fellow Americans for advice. Rarely does he directly ask his fellow Americans for advice; he simply compares notes with them on their host families and each one tries to draw some practical implications for adjusting to his own situation. This spontaneous interchange at least has therapeutic value in that the American guest finds that others are also having problems in adjusting to Colombian host families and that often what he thought was a unique behavior pattern peculiar to his host family was actually a common cultural pattern. He also discovers that some of the things he thought were cultural patterns appear to be matters of individual choice and variation.

However, we found many examples of cases where the advice one American guest had obtained from another in the spontaneous discussions at CEUCA constituted a case of "the blind leading the blind."

The basic reason for this seemed to be that the four classes of "fortuitous" factors described earlier caused the different guests to have such widely different views of certain aspects of the situation that one is reminded of the old Hindu tale of the blind men describing the elephant in which each one gives a different description depending upon which part of the elephant's anatomy he personally had felt. Each one finds it difficult to convince the other because his report runs directly counter to the other's personal experience. The problems he felt were important to deal with and the solutions he proposed depended upon which particular action pattern he had chosen as a means to the end of obtaining a hot bath, which one of the cultural alternatives his particular family followed, what information he had stumbled upon, which false assumptions were therefore brought into play, and which false conclusions were derived to act as barriers to action.

Two clearly different kinds of "miseducation" sometimes came out of this sharing. One of these reactions was for one American, after hearing of another's problem and solution, to take this solution as the proper one for his own case. Often this solution did not apply either because it was a fallacious conclusion even in the first situation or because it did not apply to the second case even though it was valid in the first situation.

The other kind of miseducation is described by one person who concluded from the discussions that, "There is no such thing as a Colombian culture pattern. As we just heard in this bull session, every Colombian family is different, so there is nothing I can learn from the others' situation that can help me to get along in my family!"

Both of these reactions seem to be based on an unconscious assumption that a culture pattern is always clear, simple, rigid, and invariable; if no such pattern is found, the behavior patterns are simply the products of the free choice of the participants. This assumption is not correct, and this makes the description of foreign cultures difficult.

Instead, a culture pattern should be conceived as a more or less stable set of alternative actions permissible in a given situation depending upon one's role in that situation. When comparing the American set of alternatives with the Colombian we can see that some alternatives are followed more frequently than others in a given culture, that some permissible alternatives in the Colombian culture are *never* permissible in the American culture. Conversely, certain permissible alternatives in the American culture are *never* permissible in the Colombian. The fact that in some situations certain alternative actions are permissible in both cultures may add to the confusion if the observer assumes, therefore, that the whole pattern is the same, or that the same variables determine which of the alternatives is permissible or preferable.

Once we attempt to objectively describe any foreign culture pattern on the basis of some systematic evidence, we are caught in the cross-cultural communication problems if we attempt to write a description to be read by members of both the guest and the host culture. If we describe the pattern in meaningful terms to the guest, these terms will be misinterpreted by the host who will feel that his culture is being inaccurately and unfairly described.

Learning the tools for cross-cultural communication

We are convinced that, in addition to providing Americans going abroad with scientifically gathered factual information relevant to the particular cultural situations, there is some hope of teaching the American certain tools and skills for discovering the relevant patterns of silent assumptions needed for successful participation and communication in the foreign culture. Of course the lone American would have to accept certain limitations since he could not be expected to accomplish what a bicultural research team could in the same setting.

Although it is beyond the scope of this book, the experiences accumulated in this field research suggest that certain tools for discovering barriers to cross-cultural communication, with or without a bicultural research team, could be developed. These tools would consist of certain skills of observation, questioning and analysis such as:

1. Learning to recognize the symptoms of miscommunication for what they are whether the symptoms are in oneself or in others.
2. Learning to separate fact, interpretation and conclusion.
3. Learning how to derive silent assumptions comprising the major premise of the interpretive process from the foreigner's minor premise and conclusion.
4. Learning how to request information from the host country citizen in such a way as not to bias or inhibit the response.

Looking to the Future

It is my conviction that the science and art of cross-cultural communication outside the field of foreign languages is in a relatively backward state. The lack of systematic empirically-based knowledge of the nonlinguistic barriers to cross-cultural communication is a pathetically weak link in our attempts at cross-cultural cooperation. Until we give serious attention to the analysis of the nonlinguistic portion of foreign cultures, as we have done over the past decades to the comparative structural analysis of languages, our attempts to build a world community free of the self-destructive effects of war, population-resource imbalance, and pollution will be seriously inhibited at the basic communication level.

At this moment in history the technological potential for international communication is increasing at a geometric rate by transporting increasing thousands of would-be communicators at supersonic speeds to bring them into face-to-face contact, and by the geometric increase in the message capacity of international communication via microwave radio and orbiting communications satellites. We should not confuse this increased amount of international *contact* with improved international *communication*.

To be sure, the amount of global interaction and interdependence is increasing, but interaction can result either in communication or miscommunication. There is no automatic assurance that the increased bombardment of messages will result in increased communication because the message may be either mere noise or communication depending upon whether the message has the same meaning for both sender and receiver. This consonance of meaning can happen only if both communicators use the same context of assumptions in interpreting the meaning of the message.

It is my hope that this modest and exploratory study will help to persuade other researchers and those upon whom we depend for financial support that this nonlinguistic and nontechnological facet of crosscultural communication is in critical need of development to balance the explosive development in the technological potential and the improvement in the teaching of foreign languages. My experience in cross-cultural research, in designing and developing international programs, and in acting as observer in United Nations specialized projects has left me with the strong conviction that of the three major links to international communication—linguistic, technological, and nonlinguistic culture patterns—the latter is the weakest and must be strengthened in all haste so that the mushroom growth in direct person-to-person contact across international boundaries will not become the means of accelerating confusion, miscommunication, and conflict.

I also hope that the basic ideas brought into focus in this project will help to persuade teachers and learners of foreign languages that they should try to incorporate as much knowledge as possible of the contemporary, operational, nonlinguistic aspects of the foreign culture into the learning of the language. Some mistakenly believe that to learn the foreign language is enough to effectively communicate. They throw in a few interesting and exotic tales about the nonlinguistic aspect of the foreign cultures merely as a bonus to motivate or provide variety or comedy-relief from the drudgery of drilling on the subjunctive. This research suggests to me that a knowledge of the nonlinguistic aspects of those situations in the foreign culture where we intend to use the language is *not* a mere frill to be tacked on when convenient. Instead, such knowledge is a basic ingredient in the cross-cultural communication process. The linguistic and the nonlinguistic aspects of the foreign culture must be integrated to maximize communication. I recognize that we social scientists have a long way to go before such functional knowledge is abundant, but if language teachers demand it, this will increase the pressure to produce it.

Notes

1. We were surprised by this after having been exposed to much more agreement on this point in Spanish grammar books.
2. Raymond L. Gorden, *Spanish Personal Names: As Barriers to Cross-Cultural Communication*, 142 pp., Mimeographed; *Initial Immersion in the Foreign Culture*, 68 pp., Mimeographed, 1968; *Contrastive Analysis of Cultural Differences which Inhibit Communication between Americans and Colombians*, 29 pp., Mimeographed, June, 1968.
3. For a systematic approach to this *semantographic analysis* see Szalay, Lorand B. and Brent, Jack E. "The Analysis of Cultural Meanings Through Free Verbal Associations," *The Journal of Social Psychology* 72 (1967): 161–87.
4. A game in which iron weights or stones are thrown with the object of hitting and discharging a piece of explosive.
5. We will use the bathing situation for illustrative purposes since it is so clear-cut.

NTC PROFESSIONAL MATERIALS

ACTFL Review

Published annually in conjunction with the American Council on the Teaching of Foreign Languages

Modern Technology in Foreign Language Education: Applications and Projects, *ed. Smith*, Vol. 19 (1989)

Modern Media in Foreign Language Education: Theory and Implementation, *ed. Smith*, Vol. 18 (1987)

Defining and Developing Proficiency: Guidelines, Implementations, and Concepts, *ed. Byrnes*, Vol. 17 (1986)

Foreign Language Proficiency in the Classroom and Beyond, *ed. James*, Vol. 16 (1984)

Teaching for Proficiency, the Organizing Principle, *ed. Higgs*, Vol. 15 (1983)

Practical Applications of Research in Foreign Language Teaching, *ed. James*, Vol. 14 (1982)

Curriculum, Competence, and the Foreign Language Teacher, *ed. Higgs*, Vol. 13 (1981)

Action for the '80s: A Political, Professional, and Public Program for Foreign Language Education, *ed. Phillips*, Vol. 12 (1980)

The New Imperative: Expanding the Horizons of Foreign Language Education, *ed. Phillips*, Vol. 11 (1979)

Building on Experience—Building for Success, *ed. Phillips*, Vol. 10 (1978)

The Language Connection: From the Classroom to the World, *ed. Phillips*, Vol. 9 (1977)

An Integrative Approach to Foreign Language Teaching: Choosing Among the Options, *eds. Jarvis and Omaggio*, Vol. 8 (1976)

Perspective: A New Freedom, *ed. Jarvis*, Vol. 7 (1975)

The Challenge of Communication, *ed. Jarvis*, Vol. 6 (1974)

Foreign Language Education: A Reappraisal, *eds. Lange and James*, Vol. 4 (1972)

Professional Resources

A TESOL Professional Anthology: Culture

A TESOL Professional Anthology: Grammar and Composition

A TESOL Professional Anthology: Listening, Speaking, and Reading

ABC's of Languages and Linguistics

Elementary Foreign Language Programs, *Gladys S. Lipton*

Award-Winning Foreign Language Programs: Prescriptions for Success, *Sims and Hammond*

Complete Guide to Exploratory Foreign Language Programs, *Kennedy and de Lorenzo*

Individualized Foreign Language Instruction, *Grittner and LaLeike*

Living in Latin America: A Case Study in Cross-Cultural Communication, *Gorden*

Oral Communication Testing, *Linder*

Practical Handbook to Foreign Language Elementary Programs, *Lipton*

Teaching Culture: Strategies for Intercultural Communication, *Seelye*

Teaching French: A Practical Guide, *Rivers*

Teaching German: A Practical Guide, *Rivers, et al.*

Teaching Spanish: A Practical Guide, *Rivers, et al.*

Transcription and Transliteration, *Wellisch*

For further information or a current catalog, write:
National Textbook Company
a division of NTC Publishing Group
4255 West Touhy Avenue
Lincolnwood, Illinois 60646-1975 U.S.A.